Florence Travel Guide 2023

Uncovering The Beauty and Secrets of Florence: A Comprehensive Guide to Italy's Artistic Jewel

Garrett Patton

Table Of Contents

6

My Experience As A Tourist In Florence

Florence, Italy. The city of Renaissance art, stunning architecture, and delicious cuisine. It's a place that leaves an indelible mark on anyone who visits, and I can attest to that.

My first time in Florence was a whirlwind of emotions, sights, and sounds. The moment I arrived at the Santa Maria Novella train station, I was struck by the grandeur of the building, the hustle and bustle of people coming and going, and the promise of adventure ahead.

I stepped out of the station and immediately found myself on the Piazza di Santa Maria Novella, surrounded by stunning architecture and lively crowds. From there, I made my way towards the heart of the city, weaving my way through narrow streets and alleys, past historic buildings and shops selling everything from gelato to leather goods.

But the real magic of Florence started to unfold as I approached the Piazza del Duomo, the beating heart of the city. There it was, the Duomo, the breathtaking cathedral that dominates the skyline of Florence. I could hardly believe my eyes. The intricate facade, the marble carvings, and the massive dome were all too much to take in at once.

I climbed the 463 steps up to the top of the dome and was rewarded with a panoramic view of Florence that took my breath away. The red-tiled roofs, the Arno river, the Ponte Vecchio, and the rolling hills beyond were all laid out before me, bathed in golden sunlight.

But Florence is not just about the Duomo and the view from its dome. There are countless other treasures to discover, such as the Uffizi Gallery, where I saw some of the most famous artworks in the world, including Botticelli's "The Birth of Venus" and da Vinci's "Annunciation." And then there's the Palazzo Pitti, with its stunning gardens and museums filled with Renaissance art and historical artifacts.

But perhaps the best part of Florence is the food. From delicious pastries and gelato to savory pasta and pizza, every meal was a delight. I still remember the incredible Florentine steak I had at Trattoria Cammillo, cooked to perfection and served with a side of roasted potatoes.

As my time in Florence drew to a close, I found myself feeling both melancholy and inspired. The beauty and history of the city had left a deep impression on me, and I knew I would never forget my first visit to this magical place.

If you're planning a trip to Italy, make sure to put Florence on your itinerary.

You won't regret it.

Chapter 1

Introduction To Florence

Brief History Of Florence

Florence, the capital city of Tuscany in Italy, has a rich history dating back to the Roman era. Over the centuries, it has been a center of trade, finance, art, and culture, and played a pivotal role in the development of the Renaissance.

The city was founded by the Etruscans in the 1st century BCE and was later conquered by the Romans. During the Roman era, Florence, then known as Florentia, was an important center of trade and commerce due to its location on the Arno River. The city remained an important economic hub during the Middle Ages, and by the 10th century, it had become a center of textile production, especially wool.

In the 13th century, Florence experienced a period of great prosperity, which was fueled by the banking industry. The city became a hub of financial activity, with the establishment of numerous banks, including the powerful Medici Bank. The Medici family, who were originally wool merchants, became the most powerful family in Florence, and their patronage of the arts and architecture helped to transform the city into a center of artistic and cultural innovation.

During the Renaissance, Florence was home to some of the most famous artists and thinkers of the time, including Leonardo da Vinci, Michelangelo, and Galileo Galilei. The Medici family, in particular, played a pivotal role in the development of the Renaissance, as they were great patrons of the arts and sciences. They commissioned many famous works of art, including Michelangelo's David and Botticelli's The Birth of Venus.

In the late 16th century, Florence came under the rule of the Grand Duchy of Tuscany, which was controlled by the Medici family. During this period, the city experienced another period of great cultural and intellectual activity, with the establishment of the Accademia della Crusca, one of the first academies of the Italian language, and the opening of the Uffizi Gallery, which is now one of the most famous art museums in the world.

In the 19th and 20th centuries, Florence continued to be an important center of culture and commerce. It was heavily bombed during World War II, but its historic center was largely preserved, and it has since become a major tourist destination, attracting millions of visitors each year.

Today, Florence is renowned for its Renaissance art and architecture, its beautiful countryside, and its rich cultural heritage. It remains one of the most important cities in Italy and is considered one of the world's great cultural centers.

Culture Of Florence

Florence, Italy is known for its rich history, stunning architecture, and breathtaking art. But beyond these world-renowned attractions, Florence also has a unique and vibrant culture that is shaped by its long history and the people who call it home.

One of the defining features of Florence's culture is its deep appreciation for the arts. This city was at the heart of the Renaissance, and it continues to be a hub of creativity and inspiration today. From the impressive collection of Renaissance art at the Uffizi Gallery to the contemporary works at the Palazzo Strozzi, Florence is a city that celebrates all forms of art. The appreciation for the arts can be seen in the city's architecture as well. From the iconic red-tiled roofs to the grand piazzas, Florence is a city that takes pride in its buildings and public spaces. The city is home to some of the most iconic landmarks in Italy, such as the Duomo, Ponte Vecchio, and

Palazzo Pitti, which have been masterfully crafted over centuries.

The city's culture is also heavily influenced by its history. Florence was once the capital of the powerful Medici family, who helped shape the city into the cultural and artistic center it is today. The Medici family's influence can be seen throughout the city, from the opulent Pitti Palace to the Medici Chapel. Their patronage of the arts and sciences helped fuel the Renaissance, and their legacy lives on in the city's museums and galleries. But while Florence may be steeped in history, it is also a modern and dynamic city. The streets are filled with stylish locals, trendy cafes, and bustling markets. The city is known for its fashion and design, with local artisans creating beautiful leather goods, jewelry, and clothing.

Florentines are also known for their passion for food and wine. The city is home to some of the best cuisine in Italy, with a focus on simple but flavorful ingredients. From the iconic bistecca alla fiorentina to the hearty ribollita soup, the local cuisine is a celebration of the region's agricultural bounty. And of course, no visit to Florence would be complete without sampling some of the local wine, such as the Chianti Classico or the Brunello di Montalcino. But beyond the art, architecture, and food, what truly makes Florence special is its people. Florentines are known for their warmth and hospitality, welcoming visitors to their city with open arms. They are proud of their heritage and eager to share it with others, whether through guided tours of historic sites or simply recommending their favorite local spots.

Florence's culture is a beautiful blend of the old and new, the artistic and practical, the historic and modern. It is a city that takes pride in its past, while also embracing the future. And it is this unique combination that makes Florence one of the most captivating and compelling destinations in the world.

Geography Of Florence

Florence, Italy, is a city that has been shaped by its geography in many ways. The city is located in central Italy, in the region of Tuscany. It sits in a valley surrounded by hills and mountains, with the Arno River running through its heart. This unique location has influenced everything from the city's history and culture to its architecture and even its cuisine. One of the most striking features of Florence's geography is its location in a valley. This has both positive and negative effects on the city. On the one hand, the valley provides a sheltered, temperate climate that makes the city a pleasant place to live and visit. On the other hand, the same valley that protects the city from harsh weather also traps pollution and can make the air quality poor.

Florence's location on the Arno River has also been important throughout the city's history. The river provided a vital transportation route for goods and people, as well as a source of power for the city's many mills and factories. Today, the river is a popular spot for tourists to take a stroll or a boat ride, and it is still an important source of water for the city.

The surrounding hills and mountains are also a defining feature of Florence's geography. These hills provide a natural barrier that has protected the city from invasion and attack for centuries. At the same time, they also make the city feel cozy and intimate, as if it is nestled in a protective embrace. The hills are also home to many of Florence's most beautiful parks, gardens, and vineyards, offering visitors and locals alike a chance to escape the bustle of the city and enjoy some fresh air and beautiful scenery.

Perhaps the most famous feature of Florence's geography is its architecture. The city is renowned for its beautiful buildings, many of which were built during the Renaissance. The use of local stone, particularly the pale pink stone known as pietra serena, gives the city a unique and cohesive look. The buildings are also designed to take advantage of the city's geography, with narrow streets winding up the hillsides and grand piazzas opening up at the bottom of the valleys. Finally, Florence's geography has also played a role in shaping its cuisine. The hills around the city are home to many small farms and vineyards that produce some of the best food and wine in Italy. The city's location on the Arno River has also made it a center for fishing, and the local cuisine reflects this with dishes like baccalà (salt cod) and trippa alla fiorentina (tripe stew).

The geography of Florence is a key factor in the city's history, culture, architecture, and cuisine. From its sheltered valley to its protective hills, the city's natural features have shaped every aspect of its character. For visitors to Florence, understanding the city's geography is essential for truly appreciating all that this beautiful and unique city has to offer.

Why Visit Florence

First of all, Florence is a city that is known for its rich artistic heritage, and it is often referred to as the birthplace of the Renaissance. This is evident in the many museums, galleries, and churches that are filled with some of the world's most incredible art and architecture. For instance, the Uffizi Gallery is home to some of the most famous paintings in history, including works by Botticelli, Leonardo da Vinci, and Michelangelo. And then there is the iconic Duomo, which is a magnificent cathedral that is a true masterpiece of engineering and design.

Another reason why Florence is worth visiting is the beauty of the city itself. The historic center of Florence is a UNESCO World Heritage site, and it's easy to see why. The streets are lined with stunning buildings and charming piazzas that are alive with activity. Walking through the city, you'll find yourself immersed in the beauty of the city's architecture, including the medieval

Ponte Vecchio Bridge that spans the Arno River. In addition to the art and architecture, Florence is also known for its incredible food and wine. The city is located in the heart of Tuscany, which is one of Italy's most famous wine regions. This means that visitors can indulge in some of the world's best wines, accompanied by delicious local cuisine. From classic Italian dishes like pizza and pasta to hearty Tuscan specialties like ribollita and bistecca alla Fiorentina, the food in Florence is truly unforgettable.

But perhaps what makes Florence truly special is the people who call it home. The Florentines are known for their warm and welcoming nature, and they take great pride in their city's history and culture. Whether you're enjoying a cup of espresso at a local cafe or chatting with a shopkeeper in a street market, you'll find that the locals are always happy to share their knowledge and passion for their city with visitors.

In conclusion, Florence, Italy is a destination that should be on everyone's travel bucket list.

From its incredible art and architecture to its beautiful streets and delicious food, Florence has something for everyone. So whether you're a history buff, a foodie, an art lover, or simply someone who appreciates the beauty of the world around you, Florence is a city that you won't want to miss.

Best Time to Visit Florence

Florence is one of the most beautiful and historic cities in Italy, known for its stunning architecture, world-class museums, and delicious cuisine. It's no wonder that millions of tourists flock to this stunning city every year, eager to soak up its rich culture and heritage. If you're planning a trip to Florence, one of the most important factors to consider is the best time to visit. While the city is a year-round destination, each season offers a different experience, and there are a few things to consider when planning your trip.

Spring (March - May)

Spring is one of the best times to visit Florence, especially if you're looking for pleasant weather and fewer crowds. The temperature ranges from 15 to 22 degrees Celsius, and the city is in full bloom with vibrant flowers and greenery. You can stroll through the beautiful gardens of Boboli or Bardini, or visit the nearby Tuscan countryside to see the olive groves and vineyards. Additionally, the Easter period in Florence is famous for its religious celebrations and processions, which are an unforgettable experience.

Summer (June - August)

Summer is peak tourist season in Florence, and for good reason. The weather is warm and sunny, perfect for sightseeing and outdoor activities. The city is alive with events and festivals, from the Festa di San Giovanni to the Estate Fiorentina. You can enjoy a gelato while walking around the historic centre, or take a dip in the Arno River to cool off. However, be prepared for long lines and crowds at the popular attractions, and higher prices for accommodations.

Autumn (September - November)

Autumn is another great time to visit Florence, as the weather is mild, and the crowds have started to thin out. The temperatures range from 12 to 20 degrees Celsius, making it a great time for outdoor activities like hiking and biking in the nearby countryside. Additionally, you can experience the harvest season in Tuscany, with local festivals and events dedicated to wine, olive oil, and truffles. The city is also at its most romantic during this time, with the changing leaves and soft light creating a magical atmosphere.

Winter (December - February)
Winter is the least popular time to visit Florence, as the weather can be cold and damp, and some attractions may be closed. However, if you're looking for a quieter and more budget-friendly experience, this is a great time to visit. The Christmas markets, decorations, and lights in the city are a sight to behold, and there are many indoor activities to enjoy, such as visiting museums and galleries or indulging in the local cuisine. Additionally, the winter season is perfect for exploring the stunning architecture of the city without the crowds.

The best time to visit Florence depends on your preferences, budget, and interests. Each season offers a unique experience, from the blooming flowers of spring to the cozy winter atmosphere. However, spring and autumn are the best times to visit, offering a balance of pleasant weather, fewer crowds, and exciting events and festivals. Whatever season you choose, you're sure to fall in love with the beauty and charm of this magnificent city.

Chapter 2

Planning Your Trip To Florence

Visas and Documentation

If you're planning a trip to Florence, Italy, it's essential to understand the visa requirements and necessary documentation to ensure a smooth and hassle-free experience. Here's everything a tourist should know about visas and documentation before visiting Florence:

Visa Requirements:

The visa requirements for Florence, Italy, will depend on your nationality and the duration of your stay. Italy is a member of the Schengen Area, a zone of 26 European countries that have abolished internal borders and allow free movement of people and goods within its territory. Citizens of certain countries, including the United States, Canada, and Australia, can travel to Italy without a visa for up to 90 days within a 180-day period for tourism or business purposes.

If you're planning to stay in Florence for more than 90 days, you'll need to obtain a long-term visa or residency permit before your trip. You can apply for a visa at the Italian embassy or consulate in your country of residence. The application process can take several weeks or even months, so it's best to apply well in advance of your planned travel dates.

Documentation:

In addition to a visa or residency permit, there are other essential documents you'll need to have with you when traveling to Florence. These include:

Passport: Your passport should be valid for at least six months beyond your intended stay in Florence. Be sure to make a photocopy of your passport and keep it separate from the original, in case of loss or theft.

Travel Insurance: It's strongly recommended to purchase travel insurance before your trip to Florence, which can help cover any unexpected medical expenses or trip cancellations.

Proof of Accommodation: You may be asked to provide proof of your accommodations in Florence, such as a hotel reservation confirmation or rental agreement.

Proof of Financial Means: You may also be required to show proof of your financial means to support your stay in Florence, such as bank statements or credit card statements.

Travel Itinerary: You should have a detailed itinerary of your trip, including transportation, accommodation, and planned activities.

Language skills: Italian is the official language in Florence, so it can be helpful to have some basic knowledge of the language, especially for communication with authorities.

Visas and documentation requirements can be complex and vary depending on your nationality and the length of your stay. It's important to do your research and ensure that you have all the necessary documents before traveling to Florence. Failure to do so can result in denied entry or even deportation. By following the guidelines and preparing in advance, you can enjoy a memorable and stress-free trip to one of the most beautiful cities in Italy.

Cost & Money

When planning a trip to Florence, it's important to consider the travel costs and money you'll need to make the most of your experience.

Here are some tips and information about travel costs and money for a trip to Florence:

Accommodation Costs: The cost of accommodation in Florence can vary widely depending on the type of hotel or accommodation you choose. Budget travelers can find hostels and budget hotels for around €20-€30 per night, while mid-range hotels can cost around €70-€100 per night. Luxury hotels can cost €200-€500 or more per night. It's important to book accommodation in advance to get the best deals.

Transportation Costs: Getting around Florence is easy and affordable. The city is relatively small and compact, and many attractions can be reached on foot. However, if you plan to visit places outside of the city, such as Pisa or Siena, you may need to take a train or bus. A single bus or tram ticket costs €1.50 and is valid for 90 minutes. A day pass costs €5 and is valid for 24 hours.

Food and Drink Costs: Italy is known for its delicious food and wine, and Florence is no exception. There are plenty of restaurants, cafes, and bars serving up traditional Tuscan cuisine, as well as international dishes. A meal at a mid-range restaurant can cost around €20-€30 per person, while a more upscale restaurant can cost €50-€100 or more per person. A glass of wine or beer typically costs around €5.

Attractions Costs: Florence is home to some of the world's most famous museums, galleries, and monuments, including the Uffizi Gallery, the Accademia Gallery, and the Duomo. Tickets to these attractions can be quite expensive, ranging from €10-€20 per person or more. It's worth booking tickets in advance to avoid long queues and save money.

Shopping Costs: Florence is famous for its high-quality leather goods, handmade paper, and artisanal crafts. If you plan to do some shopping, it's important to be aware of the prices and quality of the items you're buying. Bargaining is common in some markets and shops, but it's important to be respectful and not push too hard.

Currency: Italy uses the Euro (€) as its currency. You can exchange money at banks, exchange offices, or at ATMs, which are widely available throughout the city. Credit cards are widely accepted, but it's always a good idea to carry some cash for small purchases.

Tipping: Tipping is not expected in Italy, but it's common to round up the bill or leave a small tip if you receive good service. It's also common to leave a small tip for hotel staff, such as housekeeping.

Florence is a beautiful and historic city that offers a wide range of experiences for travelers. When planning a trip to Florence, it's important to consider the costs of accommodation, transportation, food and drink, attractions, shopping, currency, and tipping. By being aware of these costs and budgeting accordingly, you can make the most of your trip and enjoy all that Florence has to offer.

What To Pack

If you're planning a trip to Florence, Italy, there are a few things you should keep in mind when packing. Florence is a beautiful city full of history, art, and culture, and you'll want to be prepared for all the sights and experiences it has to offer. In this post, we'll cover everything a tourist should know about what to pack when planning a visit to Florence.

Clothing:
Florence has a mild Mediterranean climate, with hot summers and cool winters. The best time to visit Florence is in the spring or fall, when the temperatures are mild and the crowds are smaller. Regardless of when you visit, it's important to pack clothes that are comfortable and appropriate for the weather.

In the summer, you'll want to pack lightweight clothing such as shorts, sundresses, and t-shirts. It can get quite hot during the day, so it's important to stay cool and comfortable. However, keep in mind that many churches and museums in Florence require visitors to dress modestly, so it's a good idea to bring a light sweater or shawl to cover your shoulders and legs when necessary.

In the winter, you'll want to pack warmer clothing such as sweaters, jackets, and boots. It can get quite chilly in Florence during the winter months, so make sure to bring plenty of layers.

Footwear:
Florence is a city that's best explored on foot, so it's important to pack comfortable shoes. You'll be doing a lot of walking on uneven cobblestone streets, so it's a good idea to bring a pair of sturdy walking shoes or sneakers. If you're planning to visit any of Florence's museums or churches, keep in mind that many require visitors to wear shoes that cover the entire foot, so sandals or flip-flops may not be appropriate.

Accessories:

In addition to clothing and footwear, there are a few accessories you'll want to pack when visiting Florence. First and foremost, make sure to bring a hat and sunglasses to protect yourself from the sun. A small backpack or purse is also useful for carrying water, snacks, and other essentials while you're out and about.

Electronics:

If you plan on using your phone or other electronics while in Florence, make sure to bring a universal power adapter. The voltage in Italy is 220V, so you'll need an adapter that's compatible with this voltage. It's also a good idea to bring a portable charger to keep your phone and other devices charged while you're out and about.

Other items:

There are a few other items you'll want to pack when visiting Florence. If you plan on visiting any of Florence's museums or churches, make sure to bring a lightweight scarf or shawl to cover your shoulders and legs. You'll also want to bring a small umbrella in case of rain. Finally, don't forget to bring any necessary medication or toiletries, as these can be difficult to find in Florence.

Packing for a trip to Florence requires some careful planning, but with the right clothing, footwear, accessories, and electronics, you'll be ready to explore this beautiful city to the fullest. Whether you're strolling through the Piazza del Duomo, admiring the art at the Uffizi Gallery, or savoring a delicious gelato on the Ponte Vecchio, you'll be able to enjoy all that Florence has to offer with confidence and comfort.

How To Get To Florence

Known for its rich history, art, architecture, and stunning landscapes, Florence is a must-visit destination for anyone planning a trip to Italy. However, getting to Florence can be a bit of a challenge, especially for first-time visitors. In this post, we'll cover everything you need to know about how to get to Florence, including transportation options, routes, and tips to make your journey as smooth as possible.

By Air

If you're coming from overseas, flying to Florence's international airport, Amerigo Vespucci Airport (FLR), is the easiest and most convenient option. The airport is located just 4km northwest of the city center, making it a quick and easy journey to get to Florence. Several airlines offer direct flights to Florence, including Air France, Lufthansa, KLM, and Vueling.

From the airport, you can take a taxi, a shuttle bus, or a train to get to Florence's city center. A taxi ride takes around 15 minutes, and it costs around €25-30. A shuttle bus is a more affordable option, with tickets starting at €6. The shuttle bus takes around 25-30 minutes to reach the city center. Finally, the train is the cheapest option, with tickets starting at €1.50. The train station is located right next to the airport, and it takes around 15-20 minutes to reach Florence's central train station, Santa Maria Novella.

By Train

If you're already in Italy or Europe, traveling by train is a convenient and affordable way to get to Florence. Florence's central train station, Santa Maria Novella, is well-connected to major cities in Italy and Europe. The Italian high-speed train, Frecciarossa, connects Florence to Rome in just 1 hour and 30 minutes, Milan in 1 hour and 40 minutes, and Venice in 2 hours. You can also take a regional train from smaller towns and cities in Tuscany.

When traveling by train, it's important to book your tickets in advance, especially during peak season. You can purchase train tickets online, at the train station, or through a travel agent. If you're traveling with heavy luggage, it's important to note that there are no luggage storage facilities at Florence's central train station. However, there are luggage storage facilities located near the station.

By Bus

If you're on a tight budget, traveling by bus is a cost-effective way to get to Florence. Several bus companies operate services to Florence from major cities in Italy and Europe, including Flixbus, Eurolines, and Busitalia. The bus journey can take a bit longer than traveling by train, but it's a great way to see the Italian countryside and save some money.

By Car

Driving to Florence is a popular option for visitors who want the flexibility of traveling at their own pace. However, driving in Florence's city center can be challenging, especially during peak tourist season. If you're planning to drive to Florence, it's important to check the traffic regulations and parking rules. You'll also need to purchase a permit to enter Florence's restricted traffic zone (ZTL), which includes most of the city center.

No matter how you decide to get to Florence, here are some final tips to help make your journey as smooth as possible: If you're traveling during peak season, it's important to book your tickets and accommodations well in advance to avoid disappointment.

It's always a good idea to check the weather forecast before you travel. Florence can get quite hot during the summer months, so make sure to bring sunscreen, a hat, and plenty of water to stay hydrated. If you're traveling by train or bus, it's a good idea to arrive at the station at least 30 minutes before your departure time to avoid any last-minute rush.

If you're traveling with heavy luggage, it's important to check the luggage allowance and weight restrictions for your mode of transportation. Most trains and buses have limited space for luggage, so it's best to pack light. If you're driving to Florence, it's important to familiarize yourself with the local driving rules and regulations. Italy has strict speed limits and parking regulations, so make sure to follow them to avoid any fines.

Once you arrive in Florence, it's important to familiarize yourself with the city's public transportation system. Florence has an extensive bus network, as well as a tram system that connects the city center to the outskirts. If you're planning to visit Florence's museums and attractions, it's a good idea to purchase tickets in advance to avoid long queues. You can purchase tickets online or through a travel agent.

Getting to Florence is relatively easy, with several transportation options available. Whether you choose to fly, take the train, bus, or drive, planning ahead and familiarizing yourself with the local rules and regulations can help make your journey a smooth and enjoyable one. Once you arrive in Florence, take the time to explore the city's rich history, art, and culture, and enjoy all that this beautiful city has to offer.

Health & Safety Tips

With its rich history, stunning architecture, and world-renowned art, it's no wonder why millions of tourists flock to the city each year. But amidst all the excitement, it's important to remember to prioritize your health and safety while traveling. In this post, we'll discuss some essential health and safety tips for tourists visiting Florence.

Stay hydrated
Florence can get quite hot and humid during the summer months, so it's important to drink plenty of water to avoid dehydration. Carry a reusable water bottle with you and refill it at public drinking fountains around the city.

Wear comfortable shoes
Florence is a walking city, and you'll likely spend a lot of time on your feet exploring the city's attractions. Make sure to wear comfortable shoes that can handle lots of walking on uneven cobblestone streets.

Be aware of pickpockets

Unfortunately, pickpocketing is a common occurrence in Florence, especially in crowded tourist areas like the Uffizi Gallery and Ponte Vecchio. Keep your belongings close to you and be aware of your surroundings. Consider using a money belt or keeping valuables in a cross-body bag.

Know the emergency numbers

It's important to know the emergency numbers in case of an accident or emergency. In Italy, the emergency number is 112 for police, ambulance, or fire brigade.

Protect yourself from the sun

While you're walking around Florence, be sure to protect yourself from the sun's harmful rays. Wear sunscreen, a hat, and sunglasses to prevent sunburn and potential long-term damage.

Follow COVID-19 guidelines

Like most places around the world, Florence has implemented COVID-19 guidelines to keep tourists and locals safe. Make sure to wear a mask in indoor public spaces and follow social distancing guidelines.

Learn basic Italian phrases
While many Florentines speak English, it's always helpful to learn some basic Italian phrases to communicate with locals. This can come in handy if you need help with directions or in case of an emergency.

Be cautious when crossing the street
Italian drivers are notorious for their aggressive driving style, so be extra cautious when crossing the street. Look both ways and use pedestrian crossings when available.

Don't drink the tap water
While Florence has safe drinking water, it's recommended that tourists stick to bottled water to avoid any potential stomach issues.

Take breaks when needed

Don't push yourself too hard when exploring Florence. Take breaks when needed and rest in shaded areas to avoid exhaustion or heatstroke.

While exploring Florence can be an exciting adventure, it's important to prioritize your health and safety while traveling. By following these essential health and safety tips, you'll be able to enjoy your time in Florence while staying safe and healthy.

Chapter 3

Accomodation in Florence

Best Areas To Stay In Florence

Florence, the capital of the Tuscany region in Italy, is one of the most beautiful and historic cities in the world. It's home to an abundance of art and architecture that dates back centuries, making it a popular destination for tourists from around the globe. If you're planning a trip to Florence, it's important to know where to stay to make the most of your experience. Here are some of the best areas to stay in Florence, along with what makes them unique.

Historic Center

The Historic Center of Florence is the heart of the city and is where you'll find most of the major attractions. This area is home to the iconic Duomo, the Uffizi Gallery, and the Ponte Vecchio. If you're interested in staying in a central location and being in the middle of all the action, this is the perfect spot for you. There are plenty of hotels and apartments to choose from, with many offering views of the historic buildings and narrow streets.

Oltrarno

Located on the opposite side of the Arno River from the Historic Center, Oltrarno is a quieter and more residential area. It's a great choice for those looking for a more laid-back atmosphere while still being within walking distance of the major sights. This area is home to the Pitti Palace and the Boboli Gardens, as well as many artisan workshops and galleries. There are plenty of restaurants and bars here, but they tend to be more low-key and less touristy than those in the Historic Center.

Santa Croce

Located just east of the Historic Center, Santa Croce is known for its beautiful basilica and piazza of the same name. This area is a bit quieter than the Historic Center but still has plenty to offer. It's home to many artisan workshops and small boutiques, as well as several good restaurants and bars. The streets here are narrower and less crowded than those in the Historic Center, making it a great choice for those looking for a more authentic Italian experience.

San Lorenzo

San Lorenzo is located just north of the Historic Center and is home to the famous San Lorenzo Market. This area is a great choice for those looking to do some shopping, as there are plenty of stalls selling leather goods, souvenirs, and other items. San Lorenzo is also home to the Medici Chapel and the Basilica di San Lorenzo, making it a great choice for those interested in history and architecture.

Santo Spirito

Located on the southern side of the Arno River, Santo Spirito is another residential area with a laid-back atmosphere. It's home to the beautiful Santo Spirito church and piazza, as well as many small artisan shops and cafes. This area is a bit further from the major tourist attractions, but it's still within walking distance of most of them.

Florence offers a variety of areas to stay in depending on your preferences. Whether you're looking to stay in the middle of the action or prefer a quieter and more residential area, there's something for everyone in this beautiful city. By choosing the right area to stay in, you can make the most of your trip and have an unforgettable experience in one of the most beautiful cities in the world.

Luxury Hotels

If you're planning a trip to Florence, you'll want to stay in a comfortable and luxurious hotel that will make your stay even more enjoyable.

Here are 10 affordable luxury hotels to consider for your next visit to Florence:

Hotel Roma - $150-$300 per night
Located in the heart of Florence, the Hotel Roma is a classic Italian hotel that offers affordable luxury accommodations. With stunning views of the city, this hotel is just a short walk from some of the most popular tourist destinations in Florence.

Hotel San Giovanni - $100-$200 per night
Situated near the famous Duomo cathedral, the Hotel San Giovanni is a charming hotel that offers luxury accommodations at an affordable price. With a rooftop terrace that offers stunning

views of the city, this hotel is the perfect place to relax and unwind after a busy day of sightseeing.

Hotel Cellai - $150-$300 per night

The Hotel Cellai is a boutique hotel that offers luxury accommodations in the heart of Florence. With its elegant and sophisticated decor, this hotel is the perfect place to stay for travelers who want to experience the best of Florence.

Hotel Balestri - $150-$300 per night

Located on the banks of the Arno River, the Hotel Balestri is a luxurious hotel that offers stunning views of the city. With its comfortable accommodations and elegant decor, this hotel is the perfect place to stay for travelers who want to experience the beauty of Florence.

Hotel Cosimo de' Medici - $100-$200 per night

The Hotel Cosimo de' Medici is a charming hotel that offers affordable luxury accommodations in the heart of Florence. With its elegant decor and comfortable accommodations, this hotel is the perfect place to stay for travelers who want to experience the best of Florence.

Hotel Florence - $150-$300 per night
The Hotel Florence is a luxury hotel that offers stunning views of the city. With its comfortable accommodations and elegant decor, this hotel is the perfect place to stay for travelers who want to experience the beauty of Florence.

Hotel Albani Firenze - $100-$200 per night
The Hotel Albani Firenze is a luxurious hotel that offers affordable accommodations in the heart of Florence. With its comfortable accommodations and elegant decor, this hotel is the perfect place to stay for travelers who want to experience the best of Florence.

Hotel Art Atelier - $150-$300 per night
The Hotel Art Atelier is a charming hotel that offers luxury accommodations in the heart of Florence. With its elegant decor and comfortable accommodations, this hotel is the perfect place

to stay for travelers who want to experience the beauty of Florence.

Hotel Berchielli - $150-$300 per night

Located on the banks of the Arno River, the Hotel Berchielli is a luxurious hotel that offers stunning views of the city. With its comfortable accommodations and elegant decor, this hotel is the perfect place to stay for travelers who want to experience the best of Florence.

Hotel La Fortezza - $100-$200 per night

The Hotel La Fortezza is a charming hotel that offers affordable luxury accommodations in the heart of Florence. With its elegant decor and comfortable accommodations, this hotel is the perfect place to stay for travelers who want to experience the best of Florence.

To get to these hotels, you can take a taxi from the airport or train station. Alternatively, you can take a bus or train to the city center and walk to your hotel.

Each of these hotels offers unique benefits and experiences for travelers, making them a great choice for your stay in Florence. Some of the benefits you can expect to enjoy at these hotels include:

Stunning views - Many of these hotels offer breathtaking views of the city, including views of the Arno River, the Duomo cathedral, and other iconic landmarks.

Luxury amenities - Despite their affordable prices, these hotels offer luxurious amenities such as spa services, rooftop terraces, and elegant decor.

Convenient location - All of these hotels are located in the heart of Florence, making it easy for travelers to explore the city's many attractions.

Personalized service - Many of these hotels offer personalized service, ensuring that guests have an unforgettable experience during their stay.

Delicious cuisine - Some of these hotels offer on-site restaurants that serve delicious Italian cuisine, allowing guests to experience the city's culinary delights without having to leave their hotel.

Overall, these affordable luxury hotels are a great choice for travelers who want to experience the best of Florence without breaking the bank. From stunning views and luxurious amenities to convenient location and personalized service, these hotels have everything you need to make your stay in Florence unforgettable.

Boutique Hotels

Florence, Italy is a stunning and culturally rich city that attracts millions of tourists each year. While there are many hotels to choose from in Florence, boutique hotels are a great way to experience the city's unique charm and character.

Here are 10 affordable boutique hotels that you can stay in as a tourist visiting Florence:

Hotel Villa La Palagina: This beautiful 19th-century villa is located in the Tuscan countryside, just a short drive from Florence. The hotel offers stunning views of the surrounding hills, a swimming pool, and a restaurant that serves delicious Tuscan cuisine. Prices start at $130 per night.

Hotel Principe: This elegant hotel is located in the heart of Florence, just a few steps from the Santa Maria Novella train station. The hotel features a rooftop terrace with panoramic views of the city, a bar, and a 24-hour front desk. Prices start at $100 per night.

Hotel Lungarno: This luxury boutique hotel is located on the banks of the Arno River, in the heart of Florence's historic center. The hotel features a Michelin-starred restaurant, a rooftop bar with views of the city, and an art collection that includes works by Picasso and Cocteau. Prices start at $320 per night.

Hotel Villa Carlotta: This elegant hotel is located in the hills above Florence, just a short drive from the city center. The hotel features a swimming pool, a garden, and a restaurant that serves traditional Tuscan cuisine. Prices start at $120 per night.

Hotel Orto de' Medici: This historic hotel is located in the San Lorenzo neighborhood of Florence, just a short walk from the Duomo and the train station. The hotel features a courtyard garden, a bar, and a 24-hour front desk. Prices start at $90 per night.

Hotel Palazzo Castri 1874: This luxurious hotel is located in a historic 19th-century palace, just a short walk from the Santa Maria Novella train station. The hotel features a spa, a swimming pool, a garden, and a restaurant that serves Italian and international cuisine. Prices start at $240 per night.

Hotel Giada: This cozy hotel is located in the heart of Florence's historic center, just a short walk from the Ponte Vecchio and the Uffizi Gallery. The hotel features a rooftop terrace with panoramic views of the city, a bar, and a 24-hour front desk. Prices start at $70 per night.

Hotel Dei Macchiaioli: This historic hotel is located in a 19th-century building in the San Lorenzo neighborhood of Florence. The hotel features a courtyard garden, a bar, and a 24-hour front desk. Prices start at $100 per night.

Hotel Loggiato dei Serviti: This elegant hotel is located in a 15th-century building in the heart of

Florence's historic center, just a short walk from the Duomo and the Uffizi Gallery. The hotel features a garden terrace, a bar, and a 24-hour front desk. Prices start at $120 per night.

To get to these boutique hotels, you can fly into Florence Airport, which is located just a short distance from the city center. Alternatively, you can take a train to Florence's Santa Maria Novella train station, which is located in the heart of the city. From there, you can take a taxi or public transportation to your hotel.

Staying at these boutique hotels in Florence has many benefits. Firstly, they offer a unique and personalized experience that is tailored to the needs and preferences of each guest. The hotels are often run by owners or managers who are passionate about providing excellent service and ensuring that guests have a memorable stay.

Additionally, many of these hotels are located in historic buildings that have been beautifully restored to maintain their original charm and character. Guests can enjoy a glimpse into the city's rich cultural and architectural heritage while also enjoying modern amenities such as Wi-Fi, air conditioning, and comfortable bedding.

Another benefit of staying in these boutique hotels is their convenient location. Most of these hotels are located in the heart of Florence's historic center or within a short distance of major attractions such as the Duomo, Uffizi Gallery, and Ponte Vecchio. This makes it easy for guests to explore the city on foot and immerse themselves in its vibrant culture and history.

In terms of price, these boutique hotels offer excellent value for money. Prices range from $70 to $320 per night, depending on the hotel and the season. While some of these hotels may be more expensive than budget options, they offer a much higher level of service, comfort, and style that is well worth the investment.

If you're planning a trip to Florence, consider staying at one of these affordable boutique hotels. They offer a unique and personalized experience that combines the city's rich cultural heritage with modern amenities and excellent service. With their convenient locations, stunning architecture, and reasonable prices, these hotels are the perfect base for exploring one of Italy's most beautiful and fascinating cities.

Hostels

Florence is a popular tourist destination in Italy, known for its rich history, art, and architecture. It's not just the historic sites that draw visitors; Florence is also home to many affordable hostels where tourists can stay and enjoy their time in the city without breaking the bank. Here are five affordable hostels to consider for your next trip to Florence.

Hostel Gallo d'Oro: Located in the heart of Florence, Hostel Gallo d'Oro is a great option for travelers who want to stay in the center of the action. This hostel is just a 10-minute walk from the Florence Cathedral and the Uffizi Gallery. The hostel has dormitory-style rooms that are clean, comfortable, and affordable, with prices starting at $25 per night. The staff is friendly and helpful, and the hostel has a communal kitchen where guests can prepare their meals. To get to Hostel Gallo d'Oro, take the train to the Florence

Santa Maria Novella Station, which is a 10-minute walk away.

Plus Florence: Plus Florence is a modern and stylish hostel that offers affordable private rooms and dormitory-style rooms. This hostel has a wide range of amenities, including a swimming pool, sauna, and rooftop terrace with panoramic views of the city. The hostel is located in the heart of Florence, just a 15-minute walk from the Duomo. Prices start at $20 per night for dormitory-style rooms. To get to Plus Florence, take the train to the Florence Santa Maria Novella Station, which is a 10-minute walk away.

Hostel Archi Rossi: Hostel Archi Rossi is a charming and cozy hostel that is located just a few blocks from the Florence Santa Maria Novella Station. The hostel has private rooms and dormitory-style rooms, with prices starting at $20 per night. The hostel also offers a variety of amenities, including a bar, restaurant, and communal kitchen. The staff is friendly and helpful, and the hostel is located within walking distance of many of Florence's main attractions.

WOW Florence Hostel: WOW Florence Hostel is a modern and stylish hostel that is located just a 10-minute walk from the Florence Cathedral. The hostel has dormitory-style rooms and private rooms, with prices starting at $18 per night. The hostel has a variety of amenities, including a rooftop terrace, bar, and communal kitchen. The staff is friendly and helpful, and the hostel is located within walking distance of many of Florence's main attractions. To get to WOW Florence Hostel, take the train to the Florence Santa Maria Novella Station, which is a 10-minute walk away.

Academy Hostel: Academy Hostel is a budget-friendly hostel that is located just a few blocks from the Florence Cathedral. The hostel has dormitory-style rooms and private rooms, with prices starting at $15 per night. The hostel is clean and comfortable, and the staff is friendly and helpful. The hostel also has a communal kitchen where guests can prepare their meals. To get to Academy Hostel, take the train to the Florence Santa Maria Novella Station, which is a 10-minute walk away.

Benefits of staying in a hostel in Florence:
Staying in a hostel in Florence is a great way to save money while still enjoying all that the city has to offer. Hostels offer affordable accommodations, and many have a variety of amenities that make them comfortable and enjoyable places to stay. Hostels also offer the opportunity to meet other travelers from around the world, which can be a fun and enriching experience. Additionally, many hostels are located in central areas of the city, making it easy to explore all of Florence's main attractions.

Chapter 4

Getting Around Florence

Transportation Option

As a popular tourist destination, the city offers various transportation options to help visitors explore its beauty and heritage.

Here is everything a tourist should know about transportation options when visiting Florence:

Walking: Florence is a relatively small city, and walking is an excellent way to explore its many attractions. Visitors can take leisurely strolls through the historic streets and piazzas, enjoying the stunning architecture and beautiful views. However, be prepared for some steep hills and uneven sidewalks.

Public Transport: Florence has an extensive public transport network consisting of buses, trams, and trains. The most convenient and economical option for tourists is the bus system, which covers the entire city and its outskirts. The buses operate from 6 am to midnight, and tickets can be purchased at the bus stops, Tabacchi shops, or newspaper stands.

Taxis: Taxis are readily available in Florence and are a good option for those who don't want to walk or take public transport. However, taxis can be quite expensive, and it's always best to negotiate the fare before getting into the car. Official taxis are white with a "TAXI" sign on top, and their license number is displayed on the side of the car.

Bike Rental: Florence is a bike-friendly city, and renting a bike is a great way to explore the city and its surrounding areas. There are many bike rental shops in the city, and visitors can rent a bike for a few hours or even for an entire day. Some popular bike routes include cycling along the Arno River or through the Tuscan countryside.

Car Rental: Renting a car in Florence is not recommended, as the city's historic center is a restricted traffic zone (ZTL). Driving in the city can also be challenging due to narrow streets, limited parking, and heavy traffic. However, renting a car is a good option for those who want to explore the surrounding countryside and nearby towns.

Private Tours: Private tours are an excellent way to see Florence and its surrounding areas, especially for those who have limited time. Private tours can be tailored to the visitor's interests and preferences and can include transportation, guide services, and entrance tickets to museums and attractions.

Florence offers various transportation options for tourists to explore its beauty and heritage. Visitors can walk, take public transport, rent bikes, hire taxis, or even book private tours. It's essential to plan ahead and choose the transportation option that best suits your needs and budget. With so much to see and do in Florence, getting around the city should be a part of the adventures.

Driving in Florence

Driving in Florence can be a bit of a challenge for tourists. The city is known for its narrow streets, heavy traffic, and confusing one-way roads. However, with some preparation and caution, driving in Florence can also be a great way to explore the city and surrounding areas.

Here are some things every tourist should know about driving in Florence.

ZTL: Florence has a Zona Traffico Limitato (ZTL), which is a restricted traffic zone that covers most of the city center. The ZTL is closed to most traffic from 7:30 am to 7:30 pm Monday to Friday, and from 7:30 am to 6:00 pm on Saturdays. It's important to note that driving in the ZTL without a permit will result in a fine. If you're staying in the city center, it's best to park your car outside the ZTL and walk or take public transportation.

Limited parking: Finding parking in Florence can be challenging, especially in the city center. There are several paid parking garages throughout the city, but they can be expensive. Street parking is available but often limited and can be difficult to find. It's important to pay attention to parking signs and regulations to avoid fines.

One-way roads: Florence has many one-way streets, and it's easy to get turned around or lost. Be sure to pay attention to road signs and follow the flow of traffic. If you miss a turn, don't panic; it's usually possible to loop back around to your destination.

Driving style: Italian drivers are known for their aggressive driving style, so it's important to be alert and aware while driving in Florence. Drivers tend to drive fast, tailgate, and use their horns frequently. Don't take it personally, but also don't be afraid to use your own horn or assert yourself when necessary.

Traffic rules: Italy has a few unique traffic rules that may be different from what you're used to. For example, it's illegal to drive with your headlights off during the day, and you must carry a reflective vest and a warning triangle in your car at all times. Be sure to familiarize yourself with these rules before hitting the road.

GPS and maps: Using a GPS or a map can be very helpful when driving in Florence. However, it's important to have a reliable source, as some GPS systems may not accurately account for the ZTL or one-way roads. Consider renting a GPS system or using a trusted navigation app on your phone.

Scooters and bicycles: Florence is a popular city for scooters and bicycles, and they can be a bit of a hazard for drivers. Be sure to keep an eye out for them, especially when turning or changing lanes. It's also important to give them plenty of space when passing.

Driving in Florence can be a bit of a challenge, but it can also be a great way to explore the city and surrounding areas. Just be sure to familiarize yourself with the ZTL, parking regulations, traffic rules, and driving style before hitting the road. With some preparation and caution, you can have a safe and enjoyable driving experience in Florence.

Chapter 5

Food and Drink In Florence

Best places for Gelato, Wine, and Coffees.

Florence, the capital of Tuscany, is one of the most beautiful cities in Italy, with its stunning architecture, rich history, and vibrant culture. It's also known for its world-class cuisine, which includes some of the best gelato, wine, and coffee in the country. Whether you're a foodie or just someone who enjoys a good treat, Florence is the perfect destination for you. In this post, we'll explore some of the best places to indulge in gelato, wine, and coffee in Florence.

Gelato

Gelato is a must-try in Florence, and it's no secret that the city has some of the best gelato in the world. Here are some of the best places to try:

Gelateria dei Neri: This small gelateria is located near Santa Croce and is famous for its creamy, delicious gelato. They have a wide range of flavors, including traditional Italian flavors like stracciatella and pistachio, as well as more unique flavors like ricotta and fig.

Gelato Santa Trinita: This gelateria is located near the beautiful Ponte Santa Trinita and is a favorite among locals and tourists alike. They use only the finest ingredients, and their gelato is made fresh every day. Try their dark chocolate or salted caramel flavors for a real treat.

Vivoli: Vivoli is one of the oldest and most famous gelaterias in Florence, and it's easy to see why. Their gelato is rich, creamy, and full of flavor, and they have a wide range of flavors to choose from. Try their hazelnut or stracciatella flavors for a real treat.

Wine

Tuscany is known for its world-class wines, and Florence is no exception. Here are some of the best places to indulge in a glass (or bottle) of Tuscan wine:

Enoteca Pitti Gola e Cantina: This cozy wine bar is located near the Pitti Palace and is a great place to try a variety of Tuscan wines. They have a wide selection of wines by the glass, and their knowledgeable staff can help you choose the perfect wine to pair with your meal.

Le Volpi e l'Uva: This charming wine bar is located near the Ponte Vecchio and is a favorite among locals and tourists alike. They have an extensive wine list, and their staff is passionate about wine and eager to help you find the perfect bottle.

La Divina Enoteca: This stylish wine bar is located in the heart of Florence and is a great place to relax and enjoy a glass of wine. They have a great selection of Tuscan wines, and their food menu is also worth trying.

Coffee

Coffee is a way of life in Italy, and Florence is no exception. Here are some of the best places to enjoy a cup of coffee in Florence:

Ditta Artigianale: This trendy coffee shop has several locations throughout Florence and is known for its high-quality coffee and stylish decor. Try their cappuccino or espresso for a real treat.

La Ménagère: This unique cafe is located in a former housewares store and is now a beautiful cafe and restaurant. They have a great coffee menu, and their food is also worth trying.

Caffè Gilli: This historic cafe has been serving coffee in Florence since 1733 and is a great place to experience the city's coffee culture. Try their signature espresso or cappuccino for a taste of Florence's coffee history.

Florence is a food lover's paradise, and whether you're looking for gelato, wine, or coffee, there's something for everyone in this beautiful city. From traditional gelato shops to modern coffee houses and cozy wine bars, there are endless options to choose from. You can't go wrong with any of the places mentioned above, but don't be afraid to explore and discover new hidden gems as well. One thing to keep in mind when visiting Florence is that the best food and drink experiences are often found off the beaten path. So be sure to wander through the city's charming streets and alleys, and keep an eye out for local cafes, bars, and gelaterias that may not be as well-known as the tourist hotspots.

Additionally, it's worth noting that while Florence is a bustling city, it's still very much rooted in traditional Italian culture, which means that many shops and cafes may close for a few hours in the afternoon for the "siesta" or midday break. So plan your day accordingly and make sure to check opening hours before heading out.

Florence is a foodie's dream come true, with some of the best gelato, wine, and coffee in Italy. Whether you're strolling through the city's historic streets or enjoying a meal at a local restaurant, the rich flavors and aromas of Tuscan cuisine are sure to leave a lasting impression. So be sure to indulge in the local food and drink scene and savor every moment of your time in this beautiful city.

Traditional Tuscan Cuisines and Specialties

When it comes to Italian cuisine, Tuscany has a reputation for being a foodie's paradise. Tuscan cuisine is simple, rustic, and deeply rooted in the land and the traditions of the region. Florence, the capital city of Tuscany, is no exception. Here, visitors can find a plethora of delicious Tuscan specialties, each with its unique history and flavor.

One of the most famous Tuscan dishes is the bistecca alla Fiorentina, a thick, juicy T-bone steak that is grilled over hot coals and seasoned with nothing more than salt, pepper, and olive oil. This dish is often served with cannellini beans and a simple salad of arugula and tomatoes. The bistecca alla Fiorentina is a staple of the Florentine cuisine and has been enjoyed by locals and visitors alike for centuries.

Another must-try Tuscan specialty is the ribollita, a hearty soup made with bread, beans, and vegetables such as kale, carrots, and onions. This dish originated as a way for Tuscan peasants to use up stale bread and other leftovers, but it has since become a beloved comfort food for all. The ribollita is typically served with a drizzle of olive oil and a sprinkling of Parmesan cheese.

For those with a sweet tooth, Florence has plenty of options. One of the most famous desserts is the cantucci, a type of almond biscotti that is traditionally dipped in sweet Vin Santo wine. These crunchy biscuits are perfect for dunking and are often served at the end of a meal as a digestive. Another sweet treat to try is the schiacciata alla Fiorentina, a fluffy sponge cake that is flavored with orange zest and dusted with powdered sugar.

Of course, no trip to Florence would be complete without sampling some of the city's famous gelato. Gelato is a type of Italian ice cream that is made with milk, sugar, and natural flavorings such as fruit, nuts, or chocolate. Florence has many gelaterias, but some of the most famous are Gelateria dei Neri, Gelateria Santa Trinita, and Vivoli.

In addition to these traditional Tuscan specialties, Florence also has a thriving food scene that includes innovative restaurants, wine bars, and street food vendors. Visitors can find everything from gourmet burgers to artisanal pastries to fusion cuisine that blends Tuscan flavors with international ingredients. Florence is a food lover's paradise that offers a wide variety of traditional Tuscan cuisine and specialties. From the bistecca alla Fiorentina to the cantucci, visitors can indulge in the flavors of Tuscany and experience the region's rich culinary heritage. Whether you're a foodie or simply looking for a delicious meal, Florence is a destination that should be on every traveler's bucket list.

Top Restaurants and Trattorias in Florence

With its breathtaking views, ancient landmarks, and world-class cuisine, Florence is a favorite destination for tourists and locals alike. The city is home to some of the best restaurants and trattorias in the world, offering a wide range of culinary experiences that cater to every taste.

Here are some of the top restaurants and trattorias in Florence that you should consider visiting:

Osteria Santo Spirito - Located in the trendy Oltrarno neighborhood, Osteria Santo Spirito is known for its traditional Tuscan cuisine. The restaurant's menu is simple but delicious, featuring dishes such as homemade pasta, roasted meats, and grilled vegetables. The atmosphere is warm and welcoming, with a rustic décor that adds to the overall experience.

Trattoria Sostanza - This historic trattoria has been around since the late 1800s and is still going strong. Trattoria Sostanza is famous for its butter chicken, a dish that has been a favorite among locals and tourists alike. The restaurant's cozy atmosphere and friendly staff make it a great place to dine with friends and family.

La Giostra - Owned by the Prince of Denmark, La Giostra is a unique restaurant that combines Tuscan cuisine with a touch of royalty. The menu features dishes such as homemade pasta, roasted meats, and seafood, all served in a grand setting that includes chandeliers, frescoes, and antique furnishings.

Il Latini - This family-owned restaurant has been around since 1939 and is famous for its Florentine steak. Il Latini's menu is simple but delicious, featuring traditional Tuscan dishes such as ribollita and pappa al pomodoro. The atmosphere is lively and bustling, with long communal tables and a welcoming staff.

Cibrèo - Located in the historic Sant'Ambrogio neighborhood, Cibrèo is a top-rated restaurant that is known for its innovative take on Tuscan cuisine. The menu changes daily, depending on what ingredients are available, and features dishes such as rabbit ravioli, beef tartare, and risotto with truffles. The atmosphere is elegant and refined, with a warm and welcoming staff.

Ora d'Aria - This Michelin-starred restaurant is located in the heart of Florence and offers a fine dining experience like no other. The menu features creative, contemporary takes on traditional Tuscan dishes, using only the finest ingredients. The atmosphere is elegant and sophisticated, with a minimalist décor that puts the focus on the food.

Il Santo Bevitore - This trendy trattoria is located in the heart of the Oltrarno neighborhood and is known for its inventive take on Tuscan cuisine. The menu features dishes such as pork belly with lentils, roasted pigeon, and rabbit ragout. The atmosphere is relaxed and laid-back, with a young and trendy clientele.

Buca Lapi - Located in a historic 15th-century building, Buca Lapi is one of the oldest restaurants in Florence. The menu features traditional Tuscan dishes such as ribollita, roasted meats, and homemade pasta. The atmosphere is charming and cozy, with exposed brick walls and a fireplace that adds to the overall ambiance.

In conclusion, Florence is a food lover's paradise, with a wide range of restaurants and trattorias that cater to every taste and budget. Whether you're looking for traditional Tuscan cuisine or contemporary takes on Italian classics, you'll find something to satisfy your appetite in this beautiful city. So, make sure to add some of these top restaurants and trattorias to your itinerary and enjoy the best of Florence's culinary delights.

92

Chapter 6

Top Tourist Attractions in Florence

The Duomo

The Duomo in Florence, also known as the Cathedral of Santa Maria del Fiore, is a magnificent and awe-inspiring structure that has captivated visitors for centuries. With its massive dome, intricate marble façade, and soaring bell tower, it is truly a wonder of Renaissance architecture and engineering.

Construction on the Duomo began in 1296, but it wasn't until 1436 that the dome was completed, an achievement that required great technical skill and ingenuity. The architect, Filippo Brunelleschi, designed a double-shelled dome that is still considered one of the most impressive feats of engineering in history. The outer dome is made of brick and the inner dome is made of stone, with a space between the two that allowed workers to move freely during construction.

The exterior of the Duomo is just as remarkable as the dome. The façade is made of green, pink, and white marble, arranged in intricate patterns and designs. The entrance is flanked by two bronze doors, one of which depicts scenes from the life of John the Baptist, the patron saint of Florence. Above the doors, there are three large rose windows, each with stunning stained-glass designs.

Inside the Duomo, visitors are greeted with a vast and cavernous space, filled with stunning works of art and architecture. The nave is flanked by massive columns and arches, and the floor is covered with intricate mosaics. The main altar is a magnificent work of art, surrounded by ornate carvings and sculptures.

One of the most remarkable features of the Duomo is its frescoes. The walls and ceilings of the cathedral are covered with stunning works of art, including the famous Last Judgment fresco by Giorgio Vasari and his assistants. The fresco depicts the end of the world, with Christ sitting in judgment over the souls of the dead. It is a powerful and awe-inspiring work of art that has captivated visitors for centuries.

Another notable feature of the Duomo is its bell tower, known as Giotto's Campanile. The tower was designed by the artist Giotto di Bondone and completed in 1359. It is a masterpiece of Gothic architecture, with intricate carvings and sculptures adorning its façade. Visitors can climb to the top of the tower for breathtaking views of the city of Florence and the surrounding countryside.

Overall, the Duomo in Florence is a remarkable work of art and architecture that is not to be missed. Whether you are an art lover, an architecture enthusiast, or simply someone who appreciates beauty and history, a visit to the Duomo is an unforgettable experience. From the massive dome to the intricate façade to the stunning frescoes and sculptures inside, every aspect of the cathedral is a testament to the skill and creativity of the Renaissance masters who created it.

Uffizi Gallery

One of the top tourist attractions in Florence is the Uffizi Gallery, which is a must-visit destination for any art lover.

The Uffizi Gallery is a famous art museum that is located in the heart of Florence's historic city center. It was built in the 16th century by Giorgio Vasari, a renowned Italian architect, and it was originally designed to house the offices of the Florentine magistrates. However, in the 16th century, the Medici family decided to turn the building into a museum to showcase their impressive art collection. Today, the Uffizi Gallery is one of the most visited museums in Italy, and it attracts millions of tourists every year.

The museum is home to a vast collection of artwork, with pieces from some of the most renowned artists in history, including Botticelli, Leonardo da Vinci, Michelangelo, and

Caravaggio, among many others. The collection includes some of the most famous and recognizable works of art in the world, such as Botticelli's "The Birth of Venus" and da Vinci's "Annunciation."

One of the reasons why the Uffizi Gallery is such a popular tourist attraction is because it offers visitors a unique opportunity to immerse themselves in the history and culture of Florence. The building itself is a work of art, with its stunning architecture and beautiful interior. The museum's vast collection of artwork provides visitors with a glimpse into the rich artistic heritage of Florence, and it allows them to explore the city's history and culture through its art.

Another reason why the Uffizi Gallery is such a popular tourist attraction is that it provides visitors with an opportunity to see some of the most famous and influential works of art in history. The museum's collection includes pieces from the Renaissance, Baroque, and Rococo periods, and it showcases the evolution of art over time. Visitors can see how different artists approached their work and how their styles changed over time, providing a unique insight into the history of art.

Visitors to the Uffizi Gallery can also take advantage of the museum's audio guide, which provides them with a wealth of information about the artwork on display. The audio guide is available in multiple languages, and it offers visitors a detailed look at each piece of art, its history, and its significance. This allows visitors to appreciate the artwork on a deeper level and gain a greater understanding of its cultural and historical significance.

The Uffizi Gallery is one of the top tourist attractions in Florence for a reason. It is a unique and fascinating museum that offers visitors a glimpse into the rich artistic heritage of Florence and the world. Whether you are an art lover or simply someone who appreciates culture and history, the Uffizi Gallery is a must-visit destination that you should not miss.

Accademia Gallery

Nestled in the heart of Florence, Italy, the Accademia Gallery is a must-see destination for anyone visiting this stunning city. With its impressive collection of artworks, sculptures, and historical artifacts, the Accademia Gallery has become one of the top tourist attractions in Florence, drawing visitors from all over the world.

Founded in 1784, the Accademia Gallery was initially established as an academy of art for students to hone their skills in painting, sculpture, and architecture. Today, it is home to some of the most famous works of art from the Italian Renaissance, including Michelangelo's David, which is undoubtedly the museum's star attraction.

Michelangelo's David is a masterpiece of Renaissance sculpture that was completed in 1504. The sculpture depicts the biblical hero

David, who famously defeated the giant Goliath with just a sling and a stone. The statue stands at an impressive 17 feet tall, and its detail and craftsmanship are awe-inspiring. Visitors to the Accademia Gallery can see the David up close, admiring its smooth curves and intricate details.

But the David isn't the only masterpiece on display at the Accademia Gallery. The museum's collection also includes several other works by Michelangelo, including his unfinished sculpture of the Slaves, which showcase the artist's incredible skill and artistry. Other notable works in the collection include paintings by Italian masters like Botticelli, Ghirlandaio, and Perugino.

One of the things that makes the Accademia Gallery so special is the way it showcases the evolution of Italian art over the centuries. Visitors can see the progression from medieval art to Renaissance art, with each piece in the collection telling a unique story about the history of Italian art and culture.

Beyond the art, the Accademia Gallery also has a rich history of its own. The museum is housed in a beautiful 14th-century building that was once a hospital for the poor and infirm. The building has been restored and renovated over the years to create the perfect environment for displaying priceless works of art.

In addition to its permanent collection, the Accademia Gallery also hosts temporary exhibitions that showcase the work of contemporary artists from Italy and beyond. These exhibitions provide visitors with a unique opportunity to see new and exciting works of art, as well as to learn more about the current state of the art world. Overall, the Accademia Gallery is a fascinating and inspiring destination for anyone interested in art, history, or culture. Its impressive collection of works by Michelangelo and other Italian masters make it one of the top tourist attractions in Florence, and a must-see destination for anyone visiting this beautiful city.

Palazzo Pitti and Boboli Gardens

Among the many attractions that Florence has to offer, Palazzo Pitti and Boboli Gardens are two of the most popular and captivating destinations.

Palazzo Pitti is a Renaissance palace that was built in the 15th century for the wealthy banker Luca Pitti. Over the centuries, the palace was acquired by the powerful Medici family, who expanded and renovated the building to its present grandeur. Today, the palace houses several museums, including the Palatine Gallery, which boasts a stunning collection of Renaissance art, and the Royal Apartments, which offer a glimpse into the luxurious lifestyle of the Medici rulers.

But perhaps the most enchanting feature of Palazzo Pitti is its sprawling gardens, known as the Boboli Gardens. The gardens were designed in the 16th century by Niccolò Triburgo, and were expanded and enhanced by subsequent generations of Medici rulers. The gardens cover over 45,000 square meters and include an array of fountains, sculptures, and breathtaking views of Florence.

Visitors to the Boboli Gardens can explore a wide variety of landscapes, including manicured lawns, terraced gardens, and secluded groves. The gardens are home to several notable features, such as the Grotta del Buontalenti, a man-made cave adorned with intricate frescoes and sculptures, and the Isolotto, an island in the middle of a large pond that is surrounded by lush greenery.

One of the most remarkable things about Palazzo Pitti and Boboli Gardens is how they embody the spirit of Renaissance Florence. The palace and gardens are a testament to the creativity, innovation, and refinement of the artists and architects who shaped the city during this period. At the same time, they offer a glimpse into the opulent lifestyle of the Medici rulers, who were not only patrons of the arts, but also wielded immense political power.

Today, Palazzo Pitti and Boboli Gardens continue to captivate and inspire visitors from around the world. The gardens are a tranquil oasis in the heart of bustling Florence, and offer a peaceful respite from the noise and crowds of the city. Meanwhile, the palace itself is a masterpiece of Renaissance architecture and art, and a reminder of Florence's rich cultural heritage.

Palazzo Pitti and Boboli Gardens are truly among the top tourist attractions in Florence. They offer a fascinating glimpse into the city's rich history and culture, and provide a breathtaking experience for visitors of all ages. Whether you're a lover of art, history, or simply looking to relax and soak up the beauty of Florence, Palazzo Pitti and Boboli Gardens are not to be missed.

Piazzale Michelangelo

There are countless things to do and see in this beautiful city, but one of the top tourist attractions that cannot be missed is Piazzale Michelangelo.

Located on a hill overlooking the city center, Piazzale Michelangelo offers one of the most breathtaking views of Florence. From this vantage point, visitors can see the entire city skyline, including the Duomo, Palazzo Vecchio, and the Arno river, which snakes its way through the city.

The piazza is named after the famous Renaissance sculptor Michelangelo, who is said to have designed the square. It was built in the late 19th century as part of the urban renewal of Florence and was intended to showcase the city's beauty to tourists.

To reach the piazza, visitors can take a leisurely walk up the hill, following the winding roads and stairs that lead to the top. Along the way, they can enjoy the lush gardens and trees that line the path, which provide a much-needed respite from the hustle and bustle of the city center.

Once at the top, visitors can take in the stunning views of Florence and the surrounding hills. The piazza is surrounded by a colonnade with statues of famous Florentine figures, and there is a large bronze replica of Michelangelo's David in the center of the square. In the evening, the piazza comes alive with street performers and musicians, creating a lively and vibrant atmosphere.

But Piazzale Michelangelo is more than just a scenic lookout. It is also a hub for cultural events and festivals. Throughout the year, the square hosts concerts, art exhibits, and food festivals, showcasing the best of Florence's vibrant cultural scene.

One of the most popular events is the Festa di San Giovanni, which takes place every June to celebrate Florence's patron saint. The piazza is transformed into a massive street party, with live music, fireworks, and traditional Florentine cuisine.

In addition to its stunning views and cultural events, Piazzale Michelangelo is also home to several restaurants and cafes, offering visitors the chance to relax and enjoy a meal or a drink while taking in the views. Overall, Piazzale Michelangelo is a must-visit attraction for anyone traveling to Florence. It offers a unique perspective of the city and a chance to immerse oneself in its rich cultural heritage. Whether you're a first-time visitor or a seasoned traveler, this piazza is sure to leave a lasting impression.

Ponte Vecchio

Among the many attractions that Florence has to offer, Ponte Vecchio stands out as one of the most beloved and fascinating tourist destinations in the city.

Ponte Vecchio, which literally means "old bridge," is a medieval stone arch bridge that spans the Arno River in Florence. It is believed to have been built in Roman times, although the current version dates back to the 14th century. The bridge is unique in that it is lined with shops, which are built on top of the bridge and hang over the river.

The bridge has a long and fascinating history, dating back to the Middle Ages. During this time, it was primarily used as a route for merchants and traders to cross the Arno River. However, as time went on, the bridge became home to a variety of shops, including butchers, tanners, and goldsmiths.

Today, Ponte Vecchio is famous for its many jewelry shops, which sell everything from traditional Florentine gold jewelry to modern designer pieces. The shops on the bridge are popular with tourists, who come to admire the craftsmanship and beauty of the jewelry on display.

In addition to the shops, Ponte Vecchio is also notable for its stunning views of the Arno River and the city of Florence. The bridge offers panoramic views of the city's historic architecture and beautiful landscape. Many visitors enjoy taking a leisurely stroll along the bridge, soaking up the sights and sounds of Florence.

The bridge is also home to several notable landmarks, including the Vasari Corridor. This secret passage was built in the 16th century by the famous artist and architect, Giorgio Vasari. The corridor allowed the ruling Medici family to travel between their palace and the government building without having to mix with the common people.

In addition to the Vasari Corridor, Ponte Vecchio is home to several other notable landmarks, including the Torre dei Mannelli, a medieval tower that sits at the southern end of the bridge. The tower was once used to defend the bridge from invaders and is now a popular spot for tourists to take photos.

Overall, Ponte Vecchio is one of the top tourist attractions in Florence for good reason. Its unique history, stunning views, and beautiful jewelry shops make it a must-see destination for anyone visiting the city. Whether you're interested in history, architecture, or simply soaking up the sights and sounds of Florence, Ponte Vecchio is sure to leave a lasting impression.

Basilica di Santa Croce and Bargello Museum

When it comes to tourist attractions, two places that never fail to amaze visitors are the Basilica di Santa Croce and the Bargello Museum. Both of these historic sites have a charm that draws in tourists from around the world.

The Basilica di Santa Croce, also known as the Temple of Italian Glories, is a Roman Catholic church located in the heart of Florence. The church is famous for its stunning architecture and the numerous artworks it houses, including frescoes, sculptures, and tombs of famous personalities like Michelangelo, Galileo, and Dante. Built in the 13th century, the church is an excellent example of Italian Gothic architecture. Its exterior is simple and unadorned, while the interior is awe-inspiring with its soaring arches, intricate frescoes, and colorful stained-glass windows.

But what really makes the Basilica di Santa Croce a must-visit is its rich history. The church has been a witness to significant events throughout Italian history, from the medieval times to the Renaissance period. It has played host to the likes of St. Francis of Assisi and St. Bernardino of Siena and witnessed the birth of the Renaissance movement. The Basilica di Santa Croce is an embodiment of Italian culture and history, and visitors can't help but be captivated by its grandeur.

Another popular attraction in Florence is the Bargello Museum, located in the Palazzo del Bargello. The museum is one of the oldest in Florence, and it houses an extensive collection of Renaissance and medieval sculptures, as well as Renaissance decorative arts, including textiles, ceramics, and metalwork. Visitors can marvel at masterpieces like Donatello's David, Michelangelo's Brutus, and Cellini's bronze statue of Mercury. The museum's collection is impressive, and it provides a unique insight into the evolution of Italian art and sculpture.

Apart from its artworks, the Bargello Museum is also renowned for its architecture. The Palazzo del Bargello is a striking example of Gothic architecture, with its austere exterior and spacious interior courtyard. Visitors can enjoy a breathtaking view of the city from the museum's rooftop terrace, which offers a panoramic view of Florence's stunning skyline.

Both the Basilica di Santa Croce and the Bargello Museum offer an immersive experience in Italian culture and history. These two iconic sites are a testament to the city's artistic heritage and provide visitors with a glimpse into the Renaissance era. The charm and allure of these two attractions are undeniable, making them a must-visit for any traveler who wants to explore the heart of Florence.

The Basilica di Santa Croce and the Bargello Museum are two of the top tourist attractions in Florence. They offer an incredible experience that combines architecture, art, and history in a way that is both educational and entertaining. For any traveler looking to immerse themselves in Italian culture, these two iconic sites are a must-visit.

San Lorenzo Market

One of the most visited and famous tourist attractions in the city is the San Lorenzo Market. The market, located in the heart of Florence, is a place where you can find a vast array of products ranging from local food to leather goods, souvenirs, and much more.

The market was built in the 19th century and has since been one of the most popular places for locals and tourists alike to shop. The market is divided into two parts, an outdoor market that sells food and produce, and an indoor market that sells leather goods, souvenirs, and other products.

The outdoor market is a bustling hub of activity, where you can find a wide range of fresh produce, including fruits, vegetables, meats, and cheeses. The market is a great place to try out some of the local cuisine, including Tuscan specialties such as ribollita (a hearty vegetable soup) and bistecca alla fiorentina (Florentine-style steak).

The indoor market, on the other hand, is a treasure trove of leather goods, souvenirs, and other products. Here, you can find a wide range of items, including leather bags, wallets, belts, and jackets, as well as ceramics, jewelry, and other local crafts. The vendors in the market are known for their skill and craftsmanship, and you can often watch them at work as they create their wares.

What makes San Lorenzo Market so unique is not just the products that are sold but also the atmosphere. The market is always bustling with activity, and the vendors are friendly and welcoming. The market is a great place to experience the local culture and interact with the locals. It is also a great place to people-watch, as the market is always full of interesting characters.

San Lorenzo Market is not just a place to shop but also a place to experience the history and culture of Florence. The market is located in the heart of the city, just a few blocks from the famous Duomo cathedral. The market is surrounded by historic buildings, and it is a great place to take a stroll and admire the beautiful architecture.

San Lorenzo Market is a must-visit destination for anyone traveling to Florence. It is a place where you can experience the local culture, taste the local cuisine, and shop for unique souvenirs and gifts. The market is always buzzing with activity, and it is a great place to spend a few hours or an entire day. Whether you are a seasoned traveler or a first-time visitor, San Lorenzo Market is a place that you will not want to miss.

Chapter 7

Shopping in Florence

Fashion and Leather Goods

The city is also famous for its fashion and leather goods, which attract visitors from all over the world. If you are planning a trip to Florence and want to indulge in some shopping for fashion and leather goods, there are a few things you should know.

What To Expect

Florence is home to some of the most famous fashion and leather brands in the world, including Gucci, Prada, and Salvatore Ferragamo. You can expect to find a wide range of high-end clothing, shoes, handbags, and leather goods in the city's many boutiques and shops.

However, keep in mind that these luxury brands often come with a high price tag, so be prepared to spend a significant amount of money if you want to purchase something from one of these stores. If you are on a budget, don't worry - there are plenty of other options for shopping in Florence.

Where To Shop
The most popular shopping areas in Florence are located in the historic city center, where you will find a mix of designer boutiques and local shops selling handmade leather goods. Here are some of the top places to shop for fashion and leather goods in Florence:

Via Tornabuoni: This is one of the most upscale shopping streets in Florence, lined with designer boutiques and high-end fashion brands. You'll find stores like Gucci, Prada, and Salvatore Ferragamo here, as well as some of the city's most exclusive jewelry shops.

Ponte Vecchio: This famous bridge is home to a number of jewelry shops, many of which have been in business for centuries. You'll find everything from simple silver bracelets to elaborate diamond necklaces here.

San Lorenzo Market: This bustling market is the perfect place to shop for leather goods and other souvenirs. You'll find hundreds of stalls selling everything from leather jackets and bags to handmade jewelry and ceramics.

Via del Corso: This is a popular shopping street in Florence that is home to a mix of designer boutiques and local shops. You'll find everything from high-end fashion brands to affordable clothing stores here.

Tips For Shopping
Here are some tips to keep in mind when shopping for fashion and leather goods in Florence:

Bargaining is not common in Florence, so don't expect to negotiate prices at most shops.

Make sure to check the quality of the leather before making a purchase. Some shops may try to sell you low-quality leather goods that won't last long.

Be wary of counterfeit products. If a price seems too good to be true, it probably is.

Try to shop during the off-season if possible. Prices may be lower, and the crowds will be smaller.

In conclusion, shopping for fashion and leather goods in Florence is an exciting experience that shouldn't be missed. Whether you're looking for high-end designer brands or local handmade goods, there's something for everyone in this vibrant city. Just remember to do your research, check the quality of the products, and shop smart to get the best deals.

Jewelry and Gold

Florence is known for its rich history, stunning architecture, and incredible art, but it's also a hub for jewelry and gold shopping. Whether you're in the market for a piece of jewelry to commemorate your trip or a precious gift for someone special, there are a few things you should know before you start shopping.

Know the Value of Gold
The first and most important thing to know about shopping for jewelry and gold in Florence is the value of gold. The price of gold is determined by its weight, purity, and the current market price. Before you start shopping, it's essential to understand the current market price of gold to ensure that you are getting a fair price for your purchase. You can check the current gold prices online or consult with a local jeweler to get an idea of the price range.

Visit the City's Historic Jewelry Shops

Florence is home to some of the oldest and most respected jewelry shops in the world, and a visit to these shops is a must for any tourist interested in jewelry and gold. Many of these shops have been operating for hundreds of years and have a rich history and tradition of craftsmanship. Some of the most famous historic jewelry shops in Florence include Ponte Vecchio, Giovanni Ferraris, and Damiani.

Understand the Difference Between Handmade and Machine-Made Jewelry

In Florence, you'll find both handmade and machine-made jewelry. Handmade jewelry is typically more expensive, but it also tends to be of higher quality and more unique than machine-made jewelry. Machine-made jewelry, on the other hand, is typically less expensive and more readily available. When shopping for jewelry, it's important to understand the difference between handmade and machine-made jewelry and decide which is the best fit for your budget and preferences.

Consider the Quality of the Stones

If you're shopping for jewelry with gemstones, it's important to consider the quality of the stones. The value of a gemstone is determined by its cut, clarity, color, and carat weight. Higher-quality gemstones are more valuable, but they're also more expensive. Before making a purchase, make sure to examine the gemstones carefully and ask the jeweler about their quality and value.

Beware of Counterfeit Jewelry

Unfortunately, counterfeit jewelry is a common problem in Florence, especially around popular tourist areas. To avoid purchasing counterfeit jewelry, make sure to buy from reputable shops and avoid street vendors or pop-up stalls. Reputable jewelry shops will always provide a certificate of authenticity for their products, and they'll be happy to answer any questions you have about the jewelry's quality and value.

Be Prepared to Haggle

Haggling is a common practice in Florence, especially in the city's markets and smaller shops. If you're interested in a piece of jewelry but you think the price is too high, don't be afraid to negotiate with the seller. However, it's important to be respectful and polite when haggling and to remember that the seller has a right to set their own prices.

Shopping for jewelry and gold in Florence can be an exciting and rewarding experience for tourists. By understanding the value of gold, visiting historic jewelry shops, considering the quality of the stones, avoiding counterfeit jewelry, and being prepared to haggle, you'll be well-equipped to find the perfect piece of jewelry to commemorate your trip to this beautiful city.

Clothing and Accessories

Florence, the capital city of Tuscany, is renowned for its art, history, and stunning architecture. It's also a fantastic destination for shopping enthusiasts, particularly those interested in fashion and accessories. Florence is home to a plethora of high-end boutiques, designer outlets, and local markets, making it an excellent place to shop for clothing and accessories. Here's what every tourist should know about shopping in Florence.

When to go shopping

The best time to go shopping in Florence is during the sales season, which takes place twice a year, in January and July. During these periods, you'll find discounts of up to 50% on high-end designer brands. However, if you're not in Florence during the sales season, don't worry - there are plenty of other great deals to be found year-round.

Where To Go Shopping

Florence is home to a plethora of high-end boutiques, designer outlets, and local markets. Some of the best places to go shopping in Florence include:

Via de' Tornabuoni: This is the most famous shopping street in Florence and is home to many high-end designer stores, such as Gucci, Prada, and Salvatore Ferragamo.

The Mall: This outlet mall, located just outside Florence, is home to some of the most famous Italian brands, including Armani, Bottega Veneta, and Yves Saint Laurent.

Ponte Vecchio: This historic bridge is home to many jewelry shops, making it an excellent place to find unique and beautiful pieces of jewelry.

What To Buy

When shopping in Florence, it's essential to buy items that are unique to the region. Some of the best things to buy include:

Leather goods: Florence is famous for its leather, and you can find a wide variety of leather goods, such as bags, belts, and jackets, at the local markets and boutiques.

Jewelry: Florence is home to many talented jewelry designers, and you can find unique and beautiful pieces at the shops on Ponte Vecchio.

Silk scarves: Florence is known for its silk, and you can find a wide variety of beautiful silk scarves at the local markets and boutiques.

Tuscan wines: If you're a wine lover, be sure to pick up a bottle of Chianti or Brunello di Montalcino, two of Tuscany's most famous wines.

How To Shop

When shopping in Florence, it's important to be prepared. Here are some tips to help you make the most of your shopping experience:

Dress comfortably: Wear comfortable shoes and clothing that's easy to take on and off, especially if you're planning to try on clothing.

Bargain: Bargaining is acceptable at the local markets, so don't be afraid to negotiate a better price.

Check for authenticity: If you're buying high-end designer goods, be sure to check for authenticity. Look for the brand's logo, packaging, and quality of materials.

Keep an eye on your belongings: Pickpocketing can be a problem in crowded areas, so keep an eye on your belongings and be vigilant.

Shopping for clothing and accessories in Florence is a fantastic experience for tourists.

With its high-end boutiques, designer outlets, and local markets, Florence has something for everyone. Remember to shop during the sales season, visit the famous shopping streets and markets, and buy items that are unique to the region. By following these tips, you're sure to have a successful shopping experience in Florence.

Markets and Shopping Districts

The city is also well-known for its markets and shopping districts, where tourists can find a wide variety of local products, from leather goods to art, jewelry, and food. In this post, we will cover everything a tourist should know about markets and shopping districts in Florence.

Markets in Florence:
Mercato Centrale - This is a famous indoor market located in the heart of Florence, just a few minutes away from the train station. Here you will find a vast selection of local food products, including fresh fruits and vegetables, cheese, meats, and wine. There are also several restaurants and cafes where you can taste some of the best Italian food.

San Lorenzo Market - This is an outdoor market located near the Basilica of San Lorenzo. The market is famous for its leather goods, including bags, belts, and jackets. You will also find a variety of souvenirs, including t-shirts, ceramics, and jewelry.

Sant'Ambrogio Market - This is another popular market located in the Sant'Ambrogio neighborhood. Here you will find a variety of fresh produce, meat, and fish, as well as local products like olive oil and honey.

Shopping Districts in Florence:
Via dei Tornabuoni - This is one of the most famous shopping streets in Florence. Here you will find high-end luxury brands like Gucci, Prada, and Salvatore Ferragamo, as well as local boutiques selling handmade leather goods and jewelry.

Via del Corso - This street connects Piazza del Duomo to Piazza della Signoria and is home to several high-end stores, as well as souvenir shops and art galleries.

Oltrarno - This is the historic district located on the other side of the Arno River. Here you will find artisan shops selling handmade pottery, jewelry, and textiles. This is also the perfect place to buy handmade leather goods and unique souvenirs.

Tips for Shopping in Florence:

Bargaining - Bargaining is not common in most stores and markets in Florence, so be prepared to pay the price that is listed. However, in some markets, like the San Lorenzo Market, bargaining is accepted, so feel free to negotiate the price.

Quality - When shopping for leather goods, make sure to check the quality of the product. Genuine leather should be soft to the touch, and the stitching should be even and neat.

VAT Refund - If you are a non-EU resident, you can claim a VAT refund on your purchases. Make sure to ask the store for the appropriate forms and keep all your receipts.

Timing - Most stores and markets in Florence are closed on Sundays, so plan your shopping accordingly.

In conclusion, shopping in Florence is an exciting and memorable experience that every tourist should enjoy. From the markets to the shopping districts, there is something for everyone in this beautiful city. Just remember to take your time, shop wisely, and enjoy all that Florence has to offer.

Chapter 8

Nightlife in Florence

Bars and Pubs

Florence, the capital of Tuscany, is a city known for its rich history, art, architecture, and culinary traditions. It's also home to a vibrant nightlife scene with plenty of bars and pubs to explore. Whether you're a local or a tourist, there are a few things you should know before heading out for a night on the town.

Legal Drinking Age and Opening Hours

In Italy, the legal drinking age is 18. Bars and pubs in Florence usually open in the late afternoon and stay open until 1 or 2 am. It's important to note that some bars may close for a few hours in the early evening before reopening later in the night.

Aperitivo

One of the most popular traditions in Florence is the aperitivo. This is a pre-dinner ritual that involves drinking and snacking. Aperitivo typically takes place between 6 pm and 9 pm, and many bars and pubs offer a special aperitivo menu with a selection of small bites, such as olives, cheese, cured meats, and bruschetta, served alongside a drink.

Cover Charge

Some bars and pubs in Florence may charge a cover fee, especially on weekends or for special events. This fee usually includes a drink or two, but it's always a good idea to ask what's included before paying.

Types of Bars and Pubs

Florence has a variety of bars and pubs to suit different tastes and preferences. Here are a few types you might come across:

Wine bars - Florence is in the heart of Tuscany, which is known for its wine production. Wine bars are a great place to sample some of the local varieties and learn about the winemaking process.

Cocktail bars - For those who prefer a more sophisticated drink, Florence has plenty of cocktail bars that serve classic and creative cocktails.

Irish pubs - If you're looking for a taste of home, there are a few Irish pubs in Florence that offer a wide selection of beers and traditional pub food.

Sports bars - Sports fans can catch their favorite games at one of Florence's sports bars, which typically have large TVs and a lively atmosphere.

Craft beer pubs - Craft beer has become increasingly popular in Florence, and there are now several pubs that specialize in locally brewed beer.

Etiquette

When visiting bars and pubs in Florence, it's important to follow some basic etiquette rules.

Here are a few tips:

Do not order a cappuccino or any other coffee drink after noon. Italians consider it a breakfast-only beverage.

Always greet the bartender and other patrons with a friendly "buongiorno" or "buonasera."

Tipping is not mandatory in Italy, but it's always appreciated. You can round up the bill or leave a small tip if you receive good service.

Do not stand outside the bar or pub with your drink. Italians prefer to drink and socialize inside.

Safety

While Florence is generally a safe city, it's always a good idea to take some precautions when visiting bars and pubs, especially if you're a solo traveler or a woman. Here are a few safety tips:

Always keep an eye on your drink and never leave it unattended.

Avoid accepting drinks from strangers.

Stick to well-lit and populated areas, especially when walking alone at night.

Be aware of your surroundings and trust your instincts.

In conclusion, Florence has a lively and varied nightlife scene with plenty of bars and pubs to choose from. Whether you're looking for a casual drink or a night of dancing, there's something for everyone. By following some basic etiquette and safety tips, you can have a fun and enjoyable night out in this beautiful city.

Nightclubs

If you're planning a trip to Florence and you're looking to experience the city's vibrant nightlife, you'll find a variety of nightclubs to choose from. Here's everything you need to know about Nightclubs in Florence.

The Legal Drinking Age: In Florence, the legal drinking age is 18. So, if you're over 18, you can legally drink alcohol in nightclubs and bars.

Dress Code: It's important to note that most nightclubs in Florence have a dress code. Men are expected to wear smart casual attire, while women can opt for dresses or smart casual pants outfits. Sneakers and flip flops are generally not allowed, so be sure to wear appropriate footwear.

Entrance Fees: Most nightclubs in Florence charge an entrance fee, which varies depending on the club and the night of the week. Generally, you can expect to pay between €10 and €20 to get in.

Age Restrictions: While the legal drinking age is 18, some nightclubs in Florence have age restrictions. It's best to check the club's website or call ahead to confirm the age limit.

Music: Nightclubs in Florence play a variety of music genres, from electronic dance music to hip-hop and R&B. The type of music will depend on the club and the night of the week. Some clubs even have live music performances.

Closing Time: Nightclubs in Florence typically close at 3am. However, some clubs may stay open later, especially on weekends.

Safety: As with any nightlife scene, it's important to be aware of your surroundings and take precautions to stay safe. Stick with your group of friends, don't leave your drink unattended, and be aware of pickpockets.

Popular Nightclubs in Florence to check out:

Tenax: This club is known for its electronic dance music and has been a staple of Florence's nightlife scene for over 35 years.

YAB: This club is popular among locals and tourists alike and plays a variety of music genres.

Space Club: This club is located just outside of Florence and is known for its techno and house music.

Overall, Florence's nightlife scene is vibrant and varied, offering something for everyone. Just be sure to follow the dress code, check the age restrictions, and take precautions to stay safe.

Live Music Venues

Florence, also known as Firenze, is a city renowned for its stunning architecture, rich history, and vibrant culture. For music lovers, Florence is a city that holds an abundance of live music venues that showcase the best local and international talent. From classical music to jazz, rock to pop, and everything in between, there is something for everyone in Florence's live music scene.

One of the most famous live music venues in Florence is the Teatro del Maggio Musicale Fiorentino. This stunning opera house was built in 1933 and has hosted some of the most iconic performances in the history of Italian music. With a seating capacity of over 2,000, the Teatro del Maggio is one of the largest and most prestigious music venues in Italy. The opera house hosts a wide range of events, from classical operas to contemporary music concerts, making it a must-visit destination for music lovers visiting Florence.

Another iconic live music venue in Florence is the Teatro Verdi. This theater was built in 1854 and has played host to some of the most renowned Italian and international musicians of the past two centuries. The Teatro Verdi is a stunningly beautiful venue, with ornate decorations and a warm and intimate atmosphere. The theater's schedule is always packed with a wide range of musical performances, including jazz concerts, classical music performances, and popular music shows.

For those looking for a more intimate live music experience, the Auditorium Flog is the perfect destination. This cozy venue has a capacity of just 500 people, making it the perfect setting for an up-close-and-personal concert experience. The Auditorium Flog has hosted many popular international musicians, including Arctic Monkeys, Editors, and Franz Ferdinand, and is a must-visit for those who appreciate live music in a more intimate setting.

Another popular destination for live music in Florence is the Viper Club. This venue is a multi-functional space that hosts a wide range of events, from live music concerts to art exhibitions and theater performances. The Viper Club is renowned for its eclectic music programming, with genres ranging from rock and punk to hip hop and electronic music. The venue has a capacity of around 1,000 people, making it the perfect destination for those looking for a lively and energetic atmosphere.

For those looking for a unique and unusual live music experience, the Obihall is the perfect destination. This former slaughterhouse has been transformed into a modern music venue, with a capacity of over 3,000 people. The Obihall is renowned for its exceptional acoustics, making it the perfect destination for classical music concerts, while also hosting popular music shows and theater performances. In conclusion,

Florence is a city that boasts an incredibly diverse live music scene. Whether you are a fan of classical music or popular music, Florence's live music venues have something to offer everyone. With a range of venues from intimate clubs to grand opera houses, Florence is a city that should be on every music lover's bucket list.

Chapter 9

Day Trips from Florence

Pisa

If you're planning a trip to Pisa, Italy, you should definitely consider taking a day trip to Florence. Florence is the capital of the Tuscany region, and it is home to some of the most iconic art and architecture in the world. A day trip from Pisa to Florence is the perfect way to explore the city and see all of its amazing sights.

First of all, getting from Pisa to Florence is easy. There are trains that run regularly between the two cities, and the journey takes around an hour. Once you arrive in Florence, you'll be greeted by the city's stunning architecture and charming streets. It's easy to see why Florence has been a source of inspiration for artists and writers for centuries.

One of the first places you should visit in Florence is the Uffizi Gallery. The Uffizi is one of the oldest and most famous art museums in the world, and it is home to an incredible collection of Renaissance art. You'll see works by some of the most famous artists in history, including Leonardo da Vinci, Michelangelo, and Botticelli.

After visiting the Uffizi, you should take a stroll around the city and explore some of Florence's other attractions. The Duomo, or Cathedral of Santa Maria del Fiore, is an absolute must-see. This stunning cathedral is the largest in Italy, and it's known for its beautiful dome and intricate facade. You can climb to the top of the dome for incredible views over the city.

If you're a fan of art and architecture, you should also visit the Basilica of Santa Croce. This church is home to the tombs of some of Italy's most famous artists and writers, including Michelangelo, Galileo, and Machiavelli. It's a beautiful and peaceful place to visit, and it's a must-see for anyone interested in Italian history and culture.

Of course, no trip to Florence would be complete without trying some of the city's famous food. Florence is known for its delicious cuisine, and there are plenty of amazing restaurants and cafes to choose from. You should try some of the city's traditional dishes, like bistecca alla fiorentina (a thick cut of steak) and ribollita (a hearty vegetable soup).

Before you head back to Pisa, you should take a walk across Ponte Vecchio. This iconic bridge is one of the most famous landmarks in Florence, and it's home to some of the city's most charming shops and cafes. It's the perfect place to end your day trip from Pisa, and it's a great spot to take in the beauty and history of Florence. A day trip from Pisa to Florence is a fantastic way to explore one of Italy's most beautiful and historic cities. With its stunning art, architecture, and cuisine, Florence has something for everyone, and it's a must-see destination for anyone visiting Tuscany. So if you're planning a trip to Pisa, be sure to set aside a day to discover the wonders of Florence.

Siena

If you're looking to escape the hustle and bustle of Florence for a day and explore the beauty of Tuscany, a day trip to Siena is a must. Located just an hour south of Florence, Siena is a charming medieval town that's rich in history, culture, and art. Its narrow streets, hilltop views, and historic buildings make it a popular destination for tourists from around the world.

To start your day trip from Florence to Siena, you can either rent a car, take a bus or a train. The bus and train services are frequent, and the ride takes about an hour. The journey itself is breathtaking, as you'll pass through the rolling hills and stunning vineyards of the Tuscan countryside. Upon arrival in Siena, you'll be greeted by the city's impressive medieval walls, which were built to protect the city from invaders in the 13th century.

Once inside the city walls, you'll quickly realize why Siena is considered one of Italy's most beautiful cities. The historic center of Siena is a UNESCO World Heritage Site, and it's filled with stunning Gothic architecture, narrow streets, and quaint piazzas. The Piazza del Campo is the heart of Siena and is one of Italy's most impressive public squares. It's also the site of the famous Palio di Siena, a horse race that takes place twice a year and has been a tradition in Siena since the Middle Ages.

As you explore Siena, make sure to visit the Siena Cathedral, a magnificent Gothic masterpiece that was constructed between the 12th and 14th centuries. The cathedral is adorned with some of Italy's most famous artworks, including the Piccolomini Library, which features frescoes by Pinturicchio.

If you're a history buff, a visit to the Museo Civico is a must. The museum is housed in the Palazzo Pubblico and features an extensive collection of medieval and Renaissance art. You can also climb the Torre del Mangia, which is the tallest tower in Siena and offers stunning views of the city.

Another must-see attraction in Siena is the Basilica di San Domenico, which was built in the 13th century and is home to some of the city's most important religious relics. The church's stunning interior is decorated with frescoes, sculptures, and works by some of Italy's most famous artists, including Bernini and Michelangelo.

When it comes to food, Siena is a paradise for foodies. The city is known for its delicious Tuscan cuisine, which features fresh ingredients, hearty meats, and rich sauces. Make sure to try the local specialty, pici, a type of thick spaghetti that's typically served with a meat ragù. You can also sample some of the city's famous Chianti wines, which are produced in the surrounding hills and are considered some of Italy's best.

Overall, a day trip from Florence to Siena is an unforgettable experience. From the stunning medieval architecture to the delicious food and wine, Siena is a city that's sure to leave a lasting impression. So, if you're planning a trip to Tuscany, make sure to add Siena to your itinerary. You won't be disappointed!

Chianti

If you're visiting Florence, Italy, you absolutely have to make time for a day trip to the picturesque and charming Chianti region. Just a short drive away from the bustling city, Chianti is a peaceful haven of rolling hills, sprawling vineyards, and quaint villages.

First things first, you'll need to decide how you want to get to Chianti. You can rent a car and drive yourself, or you can book a guided tour that will take care of all the logistics for you. If you're comfortable with driving in Italy and want the freedom to explore on your own schedule, renting a car is a great option. However, if you prefer to sit back, relax, and let someone else do the driving, a tour might be the way to go.

Once you arrive in Chianti, the first thing you'll notice is the stunning scenery. The hills are covered in a patchwork of vineyards, olive groves, and cypress trees, and the air is perfumed with the sweet scent of grapes. It's easy to see why this region has been beloved by artists, writers, and travelers for centuries.

One of the highlights of a day trip to Chianti is exploring the small villages that dot the countryside. Each one has its own unique character and charm, and they all offer a glimpse into traditional Tuscan life. Some of the most popular villages to visit include Greve in Chianti, Panzano, and Radda in Chianti. These villages are known for their picturesque squares, medieval architecture, and lively markets.

Of course, no trip to Chianti would be complete without sampling some of the region's famous wines. Chianti is home to some of Italy's most famous wine estates, and you'll have plenty of opportunities to taste the local vintages. You can visit wineries for tours and tastings, or you can simply stop by one of the many enoteche (wine shops) that line the streets of the villages.

If you're a foodie, you'll also love exploring the culinary delights of Chianti. The region is known for its rustic, hearty cuisine, which is based on simple, high-quality ingredients.

You can sample local specialties like ribollita (a hearty soup made with bread, beans, and vegetables), bistecca alla fiorentina (a thick, juicy steak cooked over an open flame), and pecorino cheese (a tangy sheep's milk cheese that pairs perfectly with the local wines).

One of the best ways to experience the food and wine of Chianti is by taking a cooking class or a wine tasting tour. These tours will give you a hands-on experience of the local cuisine and a chance to learn about the history and culture of the region. Overall, a day trip to Chianti is an unforgettable experience that will leave you with lasting memories of the beauty, culture, and cuisine of Tuscany.

Whether you're a wine lover, a foodie, or simply a traveler looking for a peaceful escape from the city, Chianti is the perfect destination for a day trip from Florence

Chapter 10

Practical Information for Visitors

Useful Italian Phrases

If you're planning a trip to Florence, Italy, it's always a good idea to learn some useful Italian phrases to help you navigate the city and communicate with the locals. Here are some essential phrases that you should know before your trip:

Ciao - Hello! This is a standard greeting that you can use to say hi to anyone you meet.

Buongiorno - Good morning! Use this phrase to greet someone in the morning until around 2 PM.

Buonasera - Good evening! This phrase is used to greet someone in the evening after 2 PM.

Grazie - Thank you! Always show your appreciation when someone helps you.

Prego - You're welcome! Use this phrase when someone thanks you.

Per favore - Please! Use this phrase when you are asking for something politely.

Scusi - Excuse me! Use this phrase to get someone's attention or to apologize.

Parla inglese? - Do you speak English? If you don't speak Italian, this is an important phrase to know.

Mi scusi, dove si trova...? - Excuse me, where can I find...? Use this phrase when you need directions.

Quanto costa? - How much does it cost? This phrase is essential when shopping.

Vorrei un caffe - I would like a coffee. Coffee is an essential part of Italian culture, and you will find it everywhere.

Posso avere l'acqua? - Can I have some water? This phrase is useful when you need water in a restaurant or cafe.

Dove si trova il bagno? - Where is the bathroom? This is a critical phrase to know when you need to use the restroom.

Mi scusi, potrebbe ripetere per favore? - Excuse me, could you please repeat that? If you didn't understand something, this is a useful phrase to ask for clarification.

Non capisco - I don't understand. If you are having trouble communicating, use this phrase to let the other person know.

Mi piace - I like it. Use this phrase to express your appreciation for something.

Non mi piace - I don't like it. Use this phrase to express your dislike for something.

Buon appetito - Enjoy your meal! This phrase is used to wish someone a good meal.

A presto! - See you soon! Use this phrase when saying goodbye to someone.

Learning these useful Italian phrases will help you communicate with the locals and make your trip to Florence much more enjoyable. Don't be afraid to use them and practice your Italian while you're there.

Money-saving tips for visiting Florence

Florence, the capital of Italy's Tuscany region, is a city steeped in history, culture, and art. From the breathtaking architecture of the Duomo to the stunning Uffizi Gallery, there is so much to see and do in Florence. However, traveling to such a beautiful city can often be expensive, and as a result, many tourists are hesitant to visit. Fear not, for in this post, I will be sharing some money-saving tips for visiting Florence that will allow you to enjoy all that the city has to offer without breaking the bank.

Plan Ahead and Book Early: One of the best ways to save money when visiting Florence is to plan ahead and book early. This applies to everything from flights and accommodations to tours and activities. By doing so, you will often find that prices are significantly lower than if you were to book last minute. Additionally, you will have more options available to you, which will allow you to choose the best deals.

Visit in the Off-Season: Another way to save money when visiting Florence is to travel during the off-season. The peak tourist season in Florence is during the summer months when the weather is warm and sunny. However, this is also when prices are at their highest. By visiting during the off-season, which is typically from November to February, you can save money on flights, accommodations, and activities.

Walk or Use Public Transportation: Florence is a relatively small city, and many of the main attractions are located within walking distance of each other. Therefore, instead of taking taxis or renting a car, consider walking or using public transportation, such as buses or trams. This will save you money on transportation costs, and you will also be able to see more of the city on foot.

Eat Like a Local: Florence is known for its delicious cuisine, and there are many fantastic restaurants throughout the city. However, eating out can be expensive, especially if you choose touristy restaurants. Instead, consider eating like a local and visiting markets, food trucks, and street vendors. You will find that the food is just as delicious, and often much cheaper.

Use Discount Cards: Florence offers several discount cards that can save you money on attractions, tours, and transportation. The Firenze Card, for example, provides free entry to many of the city's museums and attractions, as well as free public transportation. Additionally, the Tuscany Region Tourist Card offers discounts on a range of activities, including wine tours, bike rentals, and cooking classes.

Stay in a Hostel or Apartment: Accommodations in Florence can be expensive, especially if you are looking for a hotel in the city center. Instead, consider staying in a hostel or apartment. Hostels offer shared dormitories, as well as private rooms, and are a great option for budget-conscious travelers. Alternatively, apartments can be rented on a short-term basis and often provide more space and amenities than a hotel room.

Take Advantage of Free Attractions: Finally, there are many free attractions in Florence that you can enjoy without spending a dime. For example, you can visit the Duomo, Piazzale Michelangelo, and the Boboli Gardens for free. Additionally, many of the city's museums offer free admission on certain days of the week, so be sure to check their schedules. Traveling to Florence can be an expensive endeavor, but it doesn't have to be. By following these money-saving tips, you can enjoy all that the city has to offer without breaking the bank.

Remember to plan ahead, travel during the off-season, eat like a local, use discount cards, stay in a hostel or apartment, take advantage of free attractions, and walk or use public transportation. By doing so you will not only save money, but you will also have a more authentic and immersive experience of the city.

Florence is a place of immense beauty, history, and culture, and by being mindful of your spending, you can ensure that you make the most of your time there. It's worth noting that these tips are not just specific to Florence. They can be applied to any travel destination and can help you save money on your travels in general. By being proactive and thoughtful about your spending, you can stretch your budget further and have more memorable experiences on your trips.

Finally, don't forget to be flexible and open-minded. Sometimes, the most memorable experiences on a trip are the unexpected ones. By being open to new experiences and opportunities, you may find hidden gems that are not included in the typical tourist itinerary. So, enjoy your trip to Florence, and remember to have fun and be adventurous.

How to navigate Florence's public transportation system

If you're planning a trip to Florence, Italy, it's important to know how to navigate the city's public transportation system. While Florence is a relatively small city, its historic center can be difficult to navigate by car, making public transportation a convenient and efficient option for getting around. In this post, we'll guide you through the ins and outs of Florence's public transportation system so you can explore the city with ease.

Types of Public Transportation in Florence

Florence's public transportation system includes buses, trams, and trains. Let's take a closer look at each of these modes of transportation.

Buses
Buses are the most common form of public transportation in Florence. They operate

throughout the city and are an affordable way to get around. Florence's bus system is run by ATAF, which is the main public transportation company in the city. The buses run from early in the morning until late at night, and some routes even operate 24 hours a day.

Trams

Trams are another option for getting around Florence. There are two tram lines in the city, T1 and T2. T1 runs from the airport to the city center, while T2 runs from the city center to the surrounding suburbs. The trams run from early in the morning until late at night and are a comfortable way to get around the city.

Trains

Florence's train station, Santa Maria Novella, is located in the heart of the city and is a major hub for regional and national trains. If you're planning on exploring other parts of Italy during your trip to Florence, taking the train is a convenient option.

Navigating Florence's Public Transportation System

Now that you know the different types of public transportation in Florence, let's dive into how to navigate the system.

Buying Tickets

Before you can ride any of Florence's public transportation, you need to purchase a ticket. You can buy tickets at tobacco shops, newsstands, and vending machines located at bus and tram stops. You can also buy tickets on board buses and trams, but they cost more than if you buy them in advance.

There are different types of tickets available depending on how long you plan on using public transportation. The most common tickets are:

Single Ride: This ticket allows you to ride any bus or tram for 90 minutes from the time of validation.

24-Hour Ticket: This ticket allows you to ride any bus or tram as many times as you want within a 24-hour period.

72-Hour Ticket: This ticket allows you to ride any bus or tram as many times as you want within a 72-hour period.

Validating Tickets

Once you have your ticket, you need to validate it before boarding any bus or tram. You can do this by stamping the ticket in one of the validation machines located at bus and tram stops. If you don't validate your ticket, you risk getting fined.

Finding Your Way

Florence's public transportation system can be confusing if you're not familiar with the city. To help you find your way, you can use Google Maps or the Moovit app. These apps provide real-time information on bus and tram schedules, as well as directions on how to get from one place to another.

Tips for Riding Public Transportation in Florence

- Keep your ticket with you at all times, you may be asked to show it to a ticket inspector.
- Be aware of pickpockets, especially on crowded buses and trams.
- If you're taking the bus, enter through the front door and exit through the back door.
- If you're taking the tram, enter through any door and exit through the center door.
- Don't eat or drink on buses or trams.
- Be courteous and give up your seat to elderly or disabled passengers, as well as pregnant women and young children.
- Be prepared for delays during rush hour, as traffic can be heavy in the city center.
- If you're traveling to the airport or train station, allow plenty of time for your journey and check schedules in advance.
- If you're not comfortable speaking Italian, it's a good idea to have your destination

written down or saved in your phone to show the driver or ticket inspector.

- Consider purchasing a Firenze Card, which includes unlimited use of public transportation in addition to free admission to many museums and attractions in the city.

Navigating Florence's public transportation system can be intimidating at first, but with a little preparation and knowledge, it's a convenient and efficient way to explore the city. Remember to purchase and validate your tickets, be aware of your surroundings, and follow basic etiquette while riding buses and trams. By doing so, you'll be able to navigate the city with ease and focus on enjoying all that Florence has to offer.

Wi-Fi and Internet Access

If you're planning a trip to Florence, one of the most important things you'll need to consider is how you'll access the internet during your stay. As a tourist, you'll want to stay connected to family and friends, keep up with work or school, and be able to access important information about the city. Luckily, Florence has plenty of options for Wi-Fi and internet access.

First and foremost, many hotels in Florence offer free Wi-Fi to their guests. This is a great option if you're planning on spending a lot of time in your hotel room, or if you want to be able to access the internet from the comfort of your own space. Keep in mind, however, that not all hotels offer the same level of Wi-Fi quality, so it's important to do your research before booking.

If you're not staying in a hotel, or if you need internet access outside of your hotel room, there are several other options available. Many cafes and restaurants in Florence offer free Wi-Fi to their customers. This is a great way to stay connected while enjoying a cup of coffee or a delicious meal. Keep in mind, however, that some cafes may require a purchase in order to use their Wi-Fi, so be sure to check with the staff before settling in.

Another option for Wi-Fi in Florence is to purchase a portable Wi-Fi device or SIM card. These can be purchased at various electronics stores throughout the city, and can be a great option if you need reliable internet access while on the go. Keep in mind that purchasing a SIM card will require you to have an unlocked phone that is compatible with Italian networks.

Finally, if you're really in a bind and need internet access right away, there are several internet cafes located throughout Florence. These cafes typically charge by the hour or by the minute, and offer a reliable and fast connection. Keep in mind, however, that these cafes may be crowded or noisy, so they may not be the best option if you need to concentrate.

Overall, there are plenty of options for Wi-Fi and internet access in Florence. Whether you're staying in a hotel, grabbing a coffee at a local cafe, or purchasing a portable Wi-Fi device, you should be able to stay connected throughout your trip. And with the internet at your fingertips, you'll be able to explore all that Florence has to offer with ease.

Conclusion

Florence, the birthplace of the Renaissance, is a city that exudes beauty, culture, and history from every corner. It is a city that has inspired countless artists, poets, and writers over the centuries, and continues to do so today. From its stunning architecture and art to its delicious cuisine and vibrant nightlife, Florence has something for everyone.

The city is home to some of the most famous art collections in the world, with the Uffizi Gallery being one of the most notable. Here, visitors can admire the works of Botticelli, Michelangelo, and Leonardo da Vinci, among others. The Accademia Gallery, home to Michelangelo's David, is another must-visit attraction for art lovers.

But Florence is not just about art. The city's architecture is equally impressive, with the Duomo, or Cathedral of Santa Maria del Fiore, being one of the most iconic landmarks. Its striking dome, designed by Filippo Brunelleschi, dominates the city's skyline and is a testament to the ingenuity and skill of Renaissance architects.

The city's food is also a highlight, with traditional Tuscan dishes such as ribollita, bistecca alla fiorentina, and pappa al pomodoro being firm favorites. And of course, no visit to Florence would be complete without sampling the city's famous gelato, which can be found in countless gelaterias around the city.

But beyond its art, architecture, and cuisine, Florence has a charm that is all its own. Its narrow streets, picturesque piazzas, and bustling markets create an atmosphere that is both vibrant and intimate. And its rich history, from the Medici family to the birth of the Italian language, is palpable in every corner of the city.

In conclusion, Florence is a city that should be on every traveler's bucket list. Its art, architecture, cuisine, and history make it a unique and captivating destination that is sure to leave a lasting impression. Whether you're a first-time visitor or a seasoned traveler, Florence is a city that will continue to inspire and captivate for years to come.

185

Made in United States
Orlando, FL
02 June 2023

33751588R00102